Wilderness Pioneer

STEPHEN F. AUSTIN *of* TEXAS

OTHER BOOKS BY CAROL HOFF

Johnny Texas
(*Winner of the first Charles W. Follett Award*)

Johnny Texas on the San Antonio Road

Wilderness Pioneer

Stephen F. Austin of Texas

by Carol Hoff

ILLUSTRATED BY ROBERT TODD

Hendrick-Long Publishing Co.

DALLAS

WILDERNESS PIONEER, STEPHEN F. AUSTIN OF TEXAS BY CAROL HOFF
LIBRARY OF CONGRESS CATALOG CARD NUMBER 55-7501
ISBN NUMBER 0-937460-25-7
ISBN NUMBER 1-885777-16-7 (sc)

COVER DESIGN : JARED C. WILSON

Author's Note

When librarians suggested the need of a biography of Stephen F. Austin for boys and girls, I was only mildly interested. I knew Austin as "the Father of Texas," the first Anglo-American colonizer of Texas, the man in whose honor were named the capital of Texas, the first flagship of the Texas Navy, and many schools, colleges, and public buildings. Of his personal life I remembered nothing, but his name as a hero gave me a vague feeling of dissatisfaction, most likely left over from some schoolday history assignment.

However, with the idea of eliminating Austin as a person to write about, I began to read *The Father of Texas* by Dr. Eugene C. Barker. Before I was halfway through, I was filled with the excitement of one who discovers a rare and wonderful thing. And by the time I had completed reading the book, I knew that I wanted to tell Austin's story so that boys and girls all over the United States would come to know him not as a stuffy figure in a history book but as a man who had a great dream for the welfare of his fellowmen and in working to make that dream come true met adventure and danger, heartache and happiness.

As I read more about Austin I realized that he is not a hero of Texas alone. He is an American hero and should be known and cherished as much as Washington, Jefferson, Lincoln, and all the other great and good men who have molded our country.

"The bloodless pioneer of the wilderness," he once wrote, "like the corn and cotton he causes to spring where it never grew before, attracts little notice." But in his own case recognition of his importance has grown through the years. On the base of his statue in

Stephen F. Austin State Park is the inscription: "No other state in the union owes its existence more completely to one man than Texas does to Austin." And historians say that this one man changed the course of history for the United States and for Mexico. When he first went to Texas, it was solidly a part of Spanish Mexico, then an older and stronger nation than the United States. If his first small American colony had not been successful, if he had not decided on the Americanization of Texas, perhaps it and the other Southwestern states would still belong to Mexico.

This account of Austin's life is based on letters, journals, and reminiscences written by Austin, his family, and friends and acquaintances. Fortunately many thick volumes of these exist. I have tried to make it a true picture of Austin and his world. In a few instances there was no actual record of conversation known to have occurred. Then I have written Austin's part of the conversation by using words he wrote on the subject. But most of the conversations, such as those with the Indians, have been preserved in letters, diaries, or other writings.

Reading about Austin and his times has been a fascinating experience for me. In my study I am deeply grateful to Dr. Eugene C. Barker, author of *The Life of Stephen F. Austin* and *The Father of Texas* and editor of *The Austin Papers,* upon whose definitive work this story has been based and without which it could not have been written; to the Texas State Historical Association for the wealth of interesting material in its *Quarterly* and *Southwestern Historical Quarterly;* to Miss Llerena B. Friend, librarian at the Barker Texas History Center at the University of Texas, for her helpful interest; to Miss Emma Lee, children's librarian of the Rosenberg Library in Galveston, for first suggesting Austin as a subject; and to the many others who have given me information and encouragement.

To Charlie and Barnes

1:

Young Stephen

BRIGHT on the pages of our country's story are the names of Texas heroes: Davy Crockett, Jim Bowie, William Travis, Sam Houston. Bold, strong, laughing men, quick to fight, but quick to offer friendship, too. Big men, with big talk.

Yet the man whom Texans honor as the Father of Texas was none of these things. He was cautious instead of reckless, steadfast for peace, slender and quiet and soft-spoken.

Instead of talking big, Stephen Fuller Austin dreamed big. He dreamed great dreams of a better world and gave his life to making these dreams come true. And in doing so, he proved the strength and courage for which Texans honor him.

The capital of Texas is named for him, and in another part of the state, a county. The first flagship of the Texas Navy was christened for him. Two Texas colleges, two state schools, and many public schools in Texas bear his name and keep it alive for the young people of the state.

Historians say that Stephen Austin changed the course of history for the United States and for Mexico. When he first went to Texas, it was solidly a part of Mexico, like all the rest of the Southwest. If his first small American colony in Texas had not been successful, perhaps Texas and the other Southwestern states would still belong to Mexico.

Stephen Austin was born in Austinville, Virginia, on November 3, 1793.

At that time Texas was only a great wilderness. Endless fields of wild flowers rippled there in the spring. Grasses grew tall on the prairies. In autumn pecan trees along the river bottoms dropped their nuts, and trees in the hill country blazed with gold and purple and scarlet. And across the land roamed huge herds of buffalo and antelope, of black cattle and mustang ponies.

But in all Texas there were only a handful of people. A few thousand savage Indians roved the prairies, and a few hundred priests and soldiers lived at the missions built to Christianize the Indians. In all the vast land of Texas there were only four real towns, the little villages of Nacogdoches and San Antonio on the five-hundred-mile-long Old San Antonio Road, of Goliad at the Mission La Bahia closer to the coast, and of Laredo on the sandy banks of the Rio Grande.

In 1793, Texas was a part of Mexico, and Mexico belonged to Spain. In fact, all the land west of the Mississippi River to the Pacific Ocean belonged to Spain. East of the Mississippi was the United States. But in 1793 the United States was only four years old and was made up of only fifteen states.

George Washington was just beginning his second term as president. Robert Fulton was just beginning to draw plans for his steamboat, and Eli Whitney had just invented the cotton gin.

Stephen was four years old when his family moved to Missouri. Forty relatives, friends, and servants traveled together. Nine wagons carried their belongings, and the Austins rode in a coach drawn by four horses. They had to go almost five hundred miles, and the journey took them three and a half months.

It was a long, tiring, dangerous trip through the wilderness and across rivers, but little Stephen did not know it; for, riding in the coach with his mother and his baby sister Emily, he was cherished and protected. Sometimes he grew restless and fretful at having to sit still so long; then he would throw his toys on the ground and tease the baby.

"Mammy," said his pretty little mother, "Stephen is becoming unbearable. Take him out and let him walk until he is tired enough to sit still."

Sometimes he felt afraid, without knowing why, except that he could tell that his mother and the other grownups were nervous and excited. Sometimes his nurse would try to frighten him into obedience.

"You better not run off in those bushes," she would warn. "First thing you know, you'll be lost, and a big old Indian will get you. You be good now, or tonight a great big bear will come out of the woods and eat you up."

But his mammy could not frighten Stephen. He would toss his curly brown hair and look up at her with a twinkle in his brown eyes and ask, "Why do bears like to eat bad boys and not good boys?"

He was at the age when he asked a thousand "what's" and "why's" about every new thing he saw, and he always wanted to help the men with their work. In the evenings when they camped for the night, he raced around like a little puppy let out of a pen, getting in everyone's way until someone took him aside for a good romp.

When the travelers reached the Great Kanawha River, they loaded their belongings on flatboats and traveled the rest of the way by water, for their new home was at the Mine à Burton on the Missouri River, near the little village of Ste. Genevieve.

The Mine à Burton was a rich lead mine. In those days lead was a very important product. It was used for bullets, all sorts of pewter objects like mugs, bowls, and candlesticks, and even for roofing important buildings. Stephen's father expected to become wealthy as a result of his mining business.

They reached Ste. Genevieve on September 20, 1798, and the Austin family made their home there until Stephen's father could get the mine to working properly and build a home.

Ste. Genevieve was a town of about seven hundred people. It was the largest in Missouri except St. Louis, which had almost two thousand inhabitants. Missouri was Spanish territory, and most of the people who lived there were Spanish or French.

Several of Stephen's friends were Spanish children. He was in and out of their homes almost as much as his own, and from these warmhearted playmates he learned the Spanish way of doing things and imitated the good manners that were so important a part of their daily life.

Stephen's good times with boys his age came to an end when the Austin home at Mine à Burton was finished. At first Stephen was lonely in his new home, for there were no other families living at the mine. Because the Osage Indians of that region were so unfriendly, the miners kept their families in Ste. Genevieve for safety.

But there was so much happening at the Mine à Burton that Stephen soon forgot to be lonely. One hundred and fifty men worked there, digging the lead and smelting it in the new furnace. Besides, Stephen's father was building a sawmill and a flour mill and was running a store. Here settlers from miles around came to buy supplies or to trade lead, furs, eggs, or vegetables for cloth or furniture or tools.

If the miners and builders were too busy to answer Stephen's questions, a trader or trapper dropping in at the store would have an amazing tale to tell. There was always someone interesting to talk to and something exciting for a boy to watch.

Moses Austin had built the largest, most comfortable home in the settlement. It was a big, rambling two-story house, not a log cabin like most of the others nearby, but a frame house made of hand-hewn lumber, strong and substantial. There were blinds at the windows and a gallery with pillars in front, and the house was set among tall trees. Stephen's father named it Durham Hall in memory of the Connecticut home of his youth.

All the settlers in that region had to be constantly on guard against the fierce Osage Indians, and lately there had been reports of several attacks on lonely cabins. One day Moses Austin came home in the middle of the afternoon. Nine-year-old Stephen could tell by his father's grim look that something was wrong, and so could his mother. "What is wrong, Moses?" she asked quickly.

"Indians," he replied.

"Indians!"

"A message from Ste. Genevieve says they're planning to attack tonight."

"Have you sent to Ste. Genevieve for help?"

"Yes, but the men there refuse to come."

"What shall we do?"

"We must get ready to defend our home."

"What shall I do, Moses?" Maria said.

"You must keep the children with you, and get food ready. Most likely the attack will be defeated tonight, but we must prepare to defend Durham Hall for several days if it should be necessary."

"How many men will help us?"

"About a dozen."

"We must get hams from the storeroom," she said quietly, "and potatoes and plenty of water. We'll carry all our tubs inside and fill them with drinking water."

"Yes, and Stephen can help with that. When the men come, I want them to carry in buckets of sand. We shall need sand to put out fires if the Indians shoot flaming arrows."

Filled with excitement, Stephen went to work. Soon the men came, and the younger ones ran upstairs and down again with their buckets of sand. They piled it on sheets where the danger of fire was greatest, near the window that opened over the one-story ell of the house.

The older men worked unsmiling and silent, but the younger ones shouted and joked and laughed. Stephen knew this was their way of being brave, and he laughed and shouted too, and his voice sounded shrill. Once as he ran through the kitchen, his mother stopped him. She sat down and put her arm around him and held him close. "Rest a minute," she said. "And quiet down. God is good. He will take care of us."

When supper was over, the men settled down to watch and wait. Stephen wanted to stay downstairs with them, but his father ordered him upstairs with his mother and little Emily.

Stephen, lying down with his clothes on, waited and listened. But he was so tired from running up and down stairs so often, and the lullaby Mother crooned to his baby sister was so soothing that against his will he fell asleep.

War whoops of the attacking Indians woke him. A shot from one of the defenders echoed through the house. Emily began to cry. In the confusion Stephen tried to slip downstairs, but his mother called him back.

Stephen ran to the window. He wanted to open the shutters a tiny chink to watch. "Stephen!" his mother called angrily. "Stay away from the windows! Behave yourself! I have enough trouble with little Emily."

Stephen went to the hall and leaned over the banister, trying to see the men. But it was like looking into a well of darkness. He could see tiny shafts of moonlight when one of the men opened a shutter to shoot, and the flash of the shot; and that was all.

The Indians circled closer, and the shouting and the shooting merged into one big blur of hideous sound.

"Stephen," his mother called, groping for him in the darkness. She drew him into the bedroom and made him sit on the bed beside her with baby Emily. Stephen tried to sit still, but inside he felt as wriggly as a rainworm. "Why must I just sit here like a baby?" he thought. "Why can't I do something to help?"

After a long time, the war whoops grew fainter. The attacks came farther apart and then stopped entirely. The Indians had been beaten off.

When daylight came and the men were sitting around the kitchen table drinking the strong hot coffee that Maria Austin made for them, Moses Austin called to his son. "Bring me the Bible, Stephen," he said, "and my quill and ink."

Stephen brought the Bible from the parlor. Moses Austin laid it on the table and turned to the pages of family history. Everyone stopped talking and watched him as he dipped his quill into the ink and began to write.

"On 12 day May, 1802," he wrote with solemn satisfaction, "the house of Moses Austin was attacked by a body of thirty Indians, but they were repulsed by the Americans, 10 in number."

2:

Dangerous Journey

WHEN Stephen was eleven, it was time for him to go East to school. The idea was not new to him. Ever since he could remember, he had known that when he was old enough he would be sent to school in Connecticut.

But when the time came, his leaving did not seem so simple and matter of fact. It was exciting to think of the long journey through the wilderness with his father's friend, Daniel Phelps, who had agreed to take him East. But he couldn't keep a lump from his throat when he thought of how long it would be before he would see his mother and father, his sister Emily, and his baby brother, James Brown Austin, again.

He and Mr. Phelps traveled as far as Pittsburgh by water. For the second time in his life Stephen spent day after day on a

river boat, floating down the Mississippi and then poling up the
Ohio. But this time he was old enough to be interested in every
detail of the trip.

Their boat was typical of those carrying furs from Moses
Austin's store to the market in Pittsburgh. Near the front of the
bargelike boat was a shelter big enough for five men, and at the
back was the big pile of furs, or peltry. Along each side of the
boat was a walk, almost like a ladder laid flat. Along this the
men with poles walked hour after hour, pushing the boat up-

stream, bracing themselves against the runglike boards to meet the force of the current.

Often Stephen walked with them, careful not to get in the way, till he knew by heart the sound of the pole coming out of the water dripping silver in the sunlight, then plunging deep down again to make a whirling eddy.

Life on the boat grew very monotonous for Stephen. He soon found that though the men were kind to him in an offhand sort of way, they did not want to be bothered by a boy. Most of the time he sat and watched the river and the tree-lined banks slipping slowly by.

All through the day they could hear birds and see them dart from tree to tree, and sometimes they could see squirrels darting up tree trunks. Once in a while they would catch a glimpse of larger animals, a deer or a bear at the water's edge. Often Stephen would rig up a fishing line and trail it from the boat. If he was lucky, they would have fish for supper when they camped that night.

Occasionally they traveled all night, but usually they chose a place where the undergrowth was not very dense and stopped well before dark. Stephen was always glad to help make camp. He liked to swing a hatchet to clear out brush for the camping place, to cut branches to put under the blankets to make sleeping more comfortable, or to chop dry wood for the fire. After the long hours of sitting still or walking slowly back and forth on the boat, he could hardly wait for the evening when he could exercise his muscles.

Best of all were the times when the hunters of the crew
would take him along. Then there was the excitement of tracking
down a deer or a bear, the thrill of shooting to kill, and the
satisfaction of going back to camp with meat for everyone.

Sometimes they traveled through Indian country. The crew
had made the trip to Pittsburgh several times, and the men knew
where Indians might be lurking behind the green wall of trees.
Then they would travel close to the opposite bank, out of reach
of arrows. They were constantly watchful, but except for several
scares had no trouble with Indians that trip.

As the long, slow days passed, Stephen's chief entertain-
ment was listening to the tales the men told.

"It was right about here," a man would remark, "that I
seen the biggest bear I ever seen. And the fightin'est, too."

"What happened?" someone would ask, and the man was
off on his story.

"Well, it was thisaway. I'm polin' away not thinkin' much of
anythin' when all of a sudden I sees somethin' movin' on the
bank, and it's this great big whopper of a bear. He's standin'
on his hind legs reachin' for somethin' in the tree.

"I let go my pole and grab my gun. 'Watch me give him a
kick in the pants,' I says. I shoot, and the bear jumps, showin'
he's hit, but he doesn't fall down the way he's 'sposed to. No,
sir. He gives a growl like thunder and starts comin' at us —
jumps right in the water and starts swimmin'.

" 'Shoot him,' I yells, and some of the men begin pepperin'
him with lead. But does that stop him? Not so's you could no-

tice it. Those shots just make him madder'n ever. He flounders
for a minute and then comes on, thrashin' and splashin'.

"All of us is so took by surprise we just stand there with
our mouths open. There's a greenhorn aboard, and he jumps
on top of the pile of peltry and screams, 'Stop him! Stop him!
He'll eat us alive!'

"But how? Shootin's no good.

" 'Give me an ax,' I yells.

"Someone sticks an ax in my hand. By this time the var-
mint has reached the boat and is tryin' to climb on board. His
claws splinter the side rail. The men beat him off with their
poles, and he falls back in the river.

" 'Leave him be,' I yells. 'Let him come! Let him show his
head over the side of the boat, and I'll fix him!'

"They see what I mean and stand back, but believe me,
they keep their poles ready. In a minute old man bear catches
hold of the boat and starts to climb on board for a nice unfriendly visit. The minute his head shows even with the deck, I
let him have it with the blunt side of the ax, thwack! Sounds
like when you bust a melon, only a hundred times louder.

"Old man bear lets go in a hurry and sinks back in the
river. He sure is dazed. A couple of the men jump in after him,
drag him to shallow water, and finish him off.

"That night we eat broiled bear meat and honey for supper,
for it turns out what the bear was reachin' for when I first seen
him was a honey tree. Was it good! Wisht I had some right
now."

Stephen wished so, too, for most of the time their food was not very good. Breakfast was strong black coffee, dried biscuit, and greasy bacon. Lunch was almost the same, except that the bacon was cold, left over from breakfast, and there was usually a piece of sweet chocolate.

Poor food was not the only hardship of the journey. There were hard, damp places to sleep, too, with mosquitoes to fight, and sudden thunderstorms that drenched them, and long, slow rains that kept them chilled for days.

Worse than these were two feelings that Stephen could not escape. One was the tiresome sameness of being cooped up on the boat with nothing to do. The other was the constant undercurrent of fear that he soon caught from the men. They were always on guard against danger — from Indians, from wild animals, from quarrels and accidents among themselves, from the treacherous river. The men seldom spoke of danger, but Stephen could tell when it was near by their quick, cold looks, their tense movements, and their sudden flares of temper.

Worst of all for Stephen was Mr. Phelps's illness. For days he lay very sick, and there was no doctor to help him. Stephen worried about Mr. Phelps and about what would happen to him if Mr. Phelps should die. But finally Mr. Phelps began to get well, though it was a long time before he got his strength back and he still suffered from rheumatism.

Once after a hair-raising tale by one of the men, Stephen said, "I wish something exciting like that would happen to us."

"Be thankful that it hasn't," the man replied sternly, "and

pray that it don't. This is no Sunday boat ride we're on, and don't you ever forget it."

At Pittsburgh Stephen and Mr. Phelps left the boatmen, who would sell their peltry and take on a load of supplies for the store in Missouri, and then begin the long journey home. He and Mr. Phelps traveled the rest of the way to Colchester, Connecticut, by coach because of Mr. Phelps's rheumatism, stopping at inns at night instead of camping out.

Stephen was very glad to see towns and people again and was interested in every sight in the bustling villages they passed through. Pittsburgh was the largest town he had ever seen until they reached Philadelphia, then the largest city in the United States.

"I could never even have imagined a city as big and beautiful as Philadelphia," Stephen thought as they rode down the wide, brick-paved streets shaded by tall trees and admired the fine white houses set along them. He marveled at the conveniences of city life that Mr. Phelps pointed out to him, water pumps on every block and lanterns on every pump to light the way at night. Mr. Phelps had to remind him not to stare at the fashionably dressed people walking along the sidewalks or riding in splendid carriages.

At last they reached their destination, Colchester. Here Mr. Phelps turned Stephen over to the Pennimans, with whom he was to stay, and gave them a letter of instructions from Stephen's father.

"My object in sending my son Stephen to New England is
to obtain his education," Moses Austin wrote. "I therefore request that he may be placed in the best school in your country....
I wish him to be furnished with such masters and connect himself with such society as becomes a young gentleman in his situation. I also wish him to be furnished with clothing proper to
appear as becomes a gentleman."

Mrs. Penniman looked at Stephen's worn buckskins and
decided that Moses Austin had been very wise to insist on good
clothes for his son. If Stephen had appeared at school in his
frontier clothes, the city boys would almost certainly have made
fun of him, and he would have been off to a bad start. Before
she entered him in school, she took him to the best shops in town
and bought him clothes like the other boys'.

Stephen followed her in a daze of excitement. His eyes popped with amazement at the size of the stores and the luxuries he saw there. He remembered his father's store, the biggest in their part of Missouri. In comparison with the store here, it seemed very small and crude.

When Stephen was properly dressed, Mr. Penniman introduced him to Mr. John Adams, principal of Bacon Academy, the school he was to attend. Mr. Adams was a tall, handsome young man, very stern-looking but with a kindly manner. Stephen learned that he was considered one of the best teachers in the state and that the new Bacon Academy was a splendid school.

Before he had courage to enter the academy next morning, Stephen walked timidly past it under the tall trees bordering the sidewalk. He looked up at its three stories and counted its windows, eighteen across, like great eyes watching him. The school looked so big that Stephen was afraid he would get lost in it. He worried about what would be expected of him in scholarship and behavior.

After school that first lonesome day he went to his room and wrote a letter to his parents. To keep his family from knowing how homesick he felt, he told them of the hardships of his journey.

"Your troubles on your journey," his father replied, "will teach you a little of what you are to expect to meet with in life.

"Remember, my dear son," he continued, "that the present is the moment to lay the foundation for your future greatness in life; that much money must be expended before your education is finished, and that time lost can never be recalled. . . . It is small things that stamp the disposition and temper of a man, and many times boys lessen their greatness in life by small things which at the moment they think of little or no consequence."

Stephen treasured this letter and kept it always.

It didn't take Stephen long to decide that he liked Bacon Academy. He soon found that he made friends there as quickly as he had in Ste. Genevieve, and he enjoyed being one of a group of boys.

He admired and respected Mr. Adams, too, and, like the other students, imitated the principal's stately manners.

Mr. Adams usually carried a heavy ivory-headed cane, with which he gestured to emphasize a point. Many a time boys with guilty consciences would flinch as he walked by, fearing that somehow his keen eyes would see their hidden disobedience and that he would lay the cane on them.

He was strict but just and insisted that the boys in his school do their best in studies and behavior. Often Stephen, like the other boys, would have been satisfied with much less than the best, especially when the assignment was hard or the boys had some mischief or adventure in mind. Yet he was glad to accept when Mr. Adams invited him to live in the Adams home.

3:

Connecticut Cousins

MOSES AUSTIN wanted his son to know his Connecticut relatives, but Stephen made his first visit to his unknown cousins in New Haven timidly.

The cousin nearest his age, a girl, knew this, and took delight in showing her backwoods cousin the fashionable furnishings of her home.

"This is just our everyday parlor," she told Stephen as she noticed his admiring look at the beautiful, highly polished cherry furniture. "Do you have an easy chair like this in Missouri? And a cherry wood candlestand?"

"No," Stephen admitted. He thought with a swift pang of homesickness of the parlor of Durham Hall. "But we have nice things in our parlor, too. Different, but nice."

"Come into our dining room," said his cousin. "I'll show you things you've never even seen before."

Stephen followed her bashfully.

"We have two cherry sideboards," she pointed out with pride. "And look at our silver service."

It was beautiful indeed, a teapot, sugar bowl, and cream pitcher on a big silver tray, gleaming so that Stephen could see himself in the rounded surfaces.

"Look," he said, "I'm like a face on a ball, that changes when you squeeze it. Now I'm fat. Now my neck is long, like a giraffe's."

They laughed at their queer reflections, and Stephen lost his timidity.

"This is a tea caddy. It's mahogany. Everybody says it's very handsome."

"It is," Stephen agreed. "What's this? It looks like a tiny pair of tongs."

"It's a pair of silver sugar tongs," his cousin explained. "See, you pick up your lump of sugar like this and drop it into your tea."

"Let me try," Stephen said. He picked up a cube of sugar and since there was no cup of tea handy, plopped it into his cousin's mouth, and then another cube into his own.

"Come on," his guide said. "The best is in our big parlor."

The big parlor was dim and cool, its heavy, rich-colored curtains shutting out light and heat, and so splendid that without knowing it both children tiptoed and talked in whispers.

"Have you ever seen a straw floor-covering like this? It's called matting, and my brother Henry brought it all the way from China."

"Has Henry really been to China?"

"Many times. He went to sea as a cabin boy when he was twelve."

"Why do you put a rug over the matting?"

"Because it's the fashion. Besides this is a very fine Wilton rug. Step on it. Feel how soft it is? I suppose you have only braided rag rugs in Missouri."

"Yes, we have rag rugs. But they're pretty, too. And we have bearskin rugs, and they're softer than this one."

"But you don't have pictures with glass over them. It's the very latest style. See?"

They looked at each of the framed prints and the handsome coat of arms over the fireplace. When his cousin felt that Stephen was properly impressed, she said, "Now let's sneak into the kitchen and get some cookies. Then we can go outside and play."

Stephen always enjoyed his visits to his New Haven cousins. He soon grew accustomed to the magnificence of their home and planned that some day he would have one like it.

One memorable Sunday he spent with his cousin Mary Austin Holley, the charming young wife of the Reverend Mr. Holley.

He went to church with them and blushed with pleasure when she put her arm through his and introduced him to the

arriving members of the congregation. He enjoyed listening to
her gracious greeting to each new arrival, and he was very proud
to sit next to her in church.

Back at home, she put aside her dignity as the minister's
wife and laughed and joked with Stephen as if she were his age.
She fed him a delicious lunch prepared the day before and teased
him about being a poor puny boy who needed her good cooking
to fatten him up. He ate until he was afraid he would pop.

When it was time for him to catch the stagecoach back to

school, he left, promising to come again soon. But it was twenty years before he saw Mary Holley again.

Stephen made other interesting and exciting visits during his Connecticut school days. One was to the rapidly growing city of New York. Another time he and some of his schoolmates saw the strange new invention of Mr. Robert Fulton, a steamboat that moved almost by magic.

When he was twelve years old, Stephen had his picture painted for his mother, a small picture called a miniature, which he could send home easily.

Stephen felt enjoyably important each time he went to pose. He liked to dress in his best Sunday suit on a week day and put on a fresh stiffly starched white stock and ruffled shirt. As he walked over to the artist's studio, he watched for admiring glances from the people he met.

Some of the boys teased him about having his picture painted like a girl and called him pretty little Stephen. But he didn't mind, for he knew that secretly most of them wished they were having their pictures painted, too.

When the miniature was finished, Stephen was satisfied with it. He thought it made him look a little chubby and not quite old enough, but it showed his auburn hair — cut very short so that it couldn't curl — and his hazel eyes. It even showed the texture of his new suit. Father would be proud of that suit, Stephen was sure.

Stephen was happy at Bacon Academy and did well there. When he left, he received this testimonial:

"This certifies that the bearer, Stephen F. Austin, has been a member of this institution and a boarder in my family most of the time, for three years past. As a scholar he has been obedient and studious; as a boarder, unexceptionable. Having passed notably the public examinations, and having during the whole period sustained a good moral character, he is judged worthy of this honorary testimonial.— John Adams, Preceptor of Bacon Academy, Colchester, Connecticut, Jan. 7, 1808."

But much that Stephen learned in Connecticut did not come

from books. Some of it he learned from his schoolmates, boys from the finest families in New England. Some of it he learned from living in the home of the Adamses, a simple home, but one filled with the love of books and music and high ideals. Some of it he learned from his cousins. Some of it he learned in church, watching the gracious, elegantly dressed congregation and listening to the long sermons that made Duty and Integrity seem very important and beautiful and set him dreaming splendid dreams of being great and good.

But altogether he learned a way of life in which people had time to spend on books and music and beautiful things, on fashionable clothes and elaborate courtesies. A life very different from the simple life of the frontier, where people had to use all their time and strength just to make a living and keep safe.

And so, all his life after, Stephen Austin was equally at ease in a pioneer cabin or the most luxurious home.

4:

College Days

IN January, 1808, when Stephen was almost fifteen years old, he left Bacon Academy and entered Transylvania University in Lexington, Kentucky, where his sister Emily was attending boarding school.

"I desire my son Stephen to enter Transylvania University," Moses Austin wrote to his old friend Mr. Phelps, "and I wish you to engage passage for him by stagecoach. If the stage does not go to Lexington, I wish you to take him with you on your next trip."

Transylvania was a new but important university. In its ten years it had already earned a fine reputation and enrolled many students who afterwards became noted men.

There Stephen studied mathematics, geography, astronomy,

natural and moral philosophy, and history. He did well in his work and "conducted himself in an exemplary and praiseworthy manner," as his certificate from the faculty stated.

But along with his studies Stephen had a great many good times. He was popular with both boys and girls, who nicknamed him "little Stephen." Letters they wrote him after he left college teased him about the girls who liked him and referred to the fun they had together.

One of the pastimes of the boys was going to see or "calling on" the girls who attended the boarding school where Emily was enrolled or who lived in Lexington. Another interesting social affair was the singing society. A singing society was as much fun as a party, but instead of having games, the boys and girls, or young ladies and gentlemen, as they were called, played music and sang together. Stephen played the flute and often accompanied the songs.

Once in a long while they enjoyed the magic of the theater, when a company of actors put on a play. But the most important social affairs of all were the balls. Generally the ballroom was elaborately decorated with flowers and streamers and hundreds of gleaming candles, and the pretty girls, sweet music, and delicious refreshments made the dances even more magical than a play in the opera house.

There was a great deal of fun and frolic, of laughter and nonsense for Stephen and his friends in college. They were always vowing to each other that they would stop playing pranks and thinking so much about girls and good times and get down to serious study. In one letter to Stephen a friend wrote that he would not "turn fool and cabous about as formerly" but really work hard at his studies when school started again.

When Stephen received this letter, he was already working hard in his father's store, for he left the University at the end of the spring session in 1810, when he was almost seventeen. At first when he learned that he could not return to college, life at Mine à Burton seemed dismal and lonesome, for his mother had taken his sister Emily and his brother James Brown for their turn of school in the East.

Stephen was not very much interested in measuring off yards of calico, counting out candles, or weighing sugar for the customers of the store, but he was always interested in the customers themselves. There were Frenchmen, Indians, American pioneers, and once in a while a Spaniard, though Missouri was no longer Spanish territory. Each had a tale to tell of danger or hardship or humor. Stephen liked to swap yarns with them. At first he only listened as they talked of the problems of settling a new land; but as the months passed, he joined in their discussions of politics and government.

He was a dependable worker, and his father soon began giving him more and more business responsibilities. In the spring of 1812 he was given charge of taking a large cargo of lead down the Mississippi to New Orleans.

At this time Stephen was a handsome youth of eighteen. Although he was about five feet ten inches tall, he was generally considered small because his hands and feet were small and he

was very slender and graceful in his movements. He looked like a dancer, but he was as wiry and tough as any of the frontiersmen who came to his father's store. He had curly dark hair and large hazel eyes and a lively expression on his face, as if something very pleasant had just happened and an interesting adventure was just around the corner.

This trip with the lead promised to be just such an adventure, for it was filled with danger and importance.

Stephen and his father had talked of it for weeks. "You know, my son," Moses Austin had said in his dignified way, "that there is strong likelihood of war between the United States and England."

"Yes," replied Stephen. "Every boat that comes up the Mississippi brings more talk of war."

"It will be necessary for our soldiers to have a great deal of lead for bullets," his father continued. "It is my plan to get all the lead I can and send it to be sòld in New York."

"How will you send it, Father?"

"Down the Mississippi on a barge to New Orleans. There it will be loaded on a cargo ship for New York. You will go with it, of course, and arrange for the sale in New York."

"I, Father?"

"Yes, my son. It will be a big undertaking for a lad your age, but I believe you will be equal to it."

"I hope so."

"We shall plan carefully. The greatest danger, of course, is in getting the barge safely down the Mississippi. I wish you to learn all you can about navigating the river, from all the river men who stop at Ste. Genevieve. And we shall select dependable men to go with you."

Stephen learned all he could about taking a barge down the Mississippi — how to cope with the current, how to avoid sunken logs, how to land the barge, and where. At the same time his father was busy mining and buying lead.

Stephen's mother and sister were still in New York. In April his father came to him with a letter. "Your mother writes that she is much distressed for lack of money," he said. "The last cash I sent her has never reached her. She has been embarrassed to have to borrow from friends. We must start the barge with the lead at once. Even then, it will be a long time before you can sell the lead in New York and take her the money."

Stephen set out on the voyage with a high heart, realizing the dangers ahead but quietly confident. His father had written him careful instructions, and he reread them often.

"Never run late at night," his father advised, "but always make a landing under a willow point in time. It's always better to lose a few hours than be exposed at night. . . . Never trust your boat to float unless you have a man on the lookout — let this rule be always strictly observed. . . . Always put to land in winds. . . . And guard against points of islands. . . . Having observed this much, I must commit you to the care of that Being that governs us all."

Stephen reread, too, his father's instructions about clothes. He was to buy a black coat which would be suitable for New Orleans, and New York and Philadelphia as well. But he was to buy white trousers to wear only in New Orleans. Stephen agreed with his father that it was important to dress suitably and well, and he looked forward to shopping in New Orleans and to enjoying life in the city for a few days before he set sail for New York.

He had plenty of time to plan and think, for his trip to New Orleans would take four or five months. He had left the mines early in May; all went well until the last of September. Then there was a sudden unexplained accident; the boat sank, and all the lead was on the bottom of the river.

Stephen remembered the trust his father had placed in him.

He pictured his unhappy mother, far from home, waiting in vain for the money she needed so badly. He had done his best. Why should the wreck have happened to him? Why had the Being that governs us all forgotten him?

Stephen was only eighteen and very miserable over the failure of his first important venture. For a little while he wished that he had gone down with the barge. But soon he reached a decision.

"Don't feel too bad," his men consoled him. "It wasn't your fault, and no one was hurt. We're only a few days from New Orleans. We can manage to get there all right."

"But not without the lead," Stephen decided. "We must raise the lead."

"That would be too dangerous," his men objected. "It would be impossible."

"We can do it," Stephen insisted. "We must do it. Please help me plan a way."

None of the arguments of the men shook his determination. Finally they agreed to help him. It was a hard job, but by diving, prying, floating, and lifting, they managed to salvage almost all the lead and take it on to New Orleans.

And there Stephen learned that the Being that governs us all had not forgotten him. For he found that the United States and England were at war and that the English were in control of the seas. If he had reached New Orleans when he had planned and had set out for New York, he and his cargo would almost certainly have been captured by the British.

As it was, although he had to give up the trip to New York, he sold the lead at a good price and returned to his father knowing that he had served him well.

5:

New Orleans

THE next years were hard ones, not only for the Austins but for most of the people in the United States. Largely as a result of the War of 1812, business was bad. In towns and cities many people were without jobs, and in the country many farmers lost their farms because they could not pay back the money they had borrowed on them.

During this time Stephen tried many things, all of which gave him experience but little else. First he took over his father's business at the mines, which was failing, and worked very hard to get his family out of debt. "When the day arrives that the whole family are out of debt," he wrote, "I mean to celebrate it as my wedding day."

But in spite of his best efforts, that day never came. Finally he realized that the task was hopeless and decided to make a new start by pioneering farther west.

In 1819 Arkansas was opened to settlers, and Stephen joined those who poured into the new territory. He bought land in what is now the city of Little Rock and helped lay out the city. He named it Arkopolis, but this name was not popular, and soon the thriving village was again known by the name given by Indians and French explorers, Little Rock.

While he lived in Arkansas, Stephen took an active part in the affairs of the new territorry. He became an officer in the militia and was appointed a federal judge of Arkansas. He also wrote articles for the *Arkansas Gazette,* the oldest newspaper in the West.

In the meantime, Moses Austin, bitter and disappointed because he had become poor after so many years of wealth, was planning a great new venture. He had thought of a plan that would benefit many people who, like himself, were having money troubles, and at the same time make him rich again.

The plan was to get permission to settle families in Texas, where they could start anew.

Texas belonged to Mexico, and Mexico was still a part of Spain. Austin planned that the Mexican government would give the land to the new settlers from the United States, but that these settlers would pay him for doing all the necessary work so that they could get their new homes.

He tried to persuade Stephen to join him in this great undertaking, but Stephen was not enthusiastic. He was afraid that it would be just another disappointing failure for his father, like the mines and the bank he had started in New Orleans.

But Moses Austin was determined to go ahead with his plan. "To remain in a country where I had enjoyed wealth in a state of poverty," he said firmly, "I could not submit to."

So Moses Austin made the long journey through the wilderness to the little Texas village of San Antonio. But there he met disappointment. He had hoped that the Mexican officials would welcome him and approve his plan of bringing American families to settle in Texas. Instead they refused him permission.

He tried to explain how it would benefit Mexico to have settlers colonize the wild land of Texas, but they would not listen. Sick at heart, he prepared to leave.

And then by chance on Christmas Day he met Baron de Bastrop, whom he had known years before in Louisiana. Baron de Bastrop, who had become an important person in Texas, liked Austin's plan. He persuaded the Mexican officials to grant Austin permission to choose land and bring in three hundred families to settle there.

Austin left for home, full of enthusiasm and eager to find families to move to Texas. But the trip back through the wilderness was even harder than before. He and the servant who was traveling with him became ill. Their gunpowder got wet and was useless, and they could kill no game. Once they had to live on roots and acorns for eight days.

"I reached home," he wrote Stephen, "after suffering everything but death."

Excited and happy in spite of his hardships, Moses Austin worked night and day to recruit families for his Texas colony and to take them there safely. He had to plan, too, for all the supplies they would need to build their new homes and live until they could make their first crops.

In the meantime Stephen had gone to New Orleans to look for work. But there were so many other young men doing exactly the same thing that he could not find any sort of job. He did, however, find an opportunity to study law with Mr. Joseph H. Hawkins, whose brother he had known at Transylvania University.

According to the custom of the time, he would work for

Mr. Hawkins in his law office, and instead of paying him, Mr. Hawkins would teach him to become a lawyer.

"I shall earn nothing to help you with for at least eighteen months," he wrote his mother. "It will take me eighteen months to become acquainted with civil law . . . and to learn the French language — but once done I then shall have the means of fortune within my reach."

Stephen found New Orleans an interesting place to live, and he enjoyed his new work. Away from the frontier and in a city again, he had an opportunity for the things he liked most, dancing, books, music, plays and operas, and above all, the companionship of many friends.

He was twenty-six years old and felt that at last he was settled for life.

He made good progress in his law studies. In June of that year Mr. Hawkins wrote his mother, "Your son Stephen F. Austin has been a member of my family for the last eight months. His admirable qualities of the heart combined with his intelligence and acquirements will always secure him friends."

But Stephen's pleasant new life was interrupted by a message from his father.

Having completed his plans to return to Texas, Moses Austin went to visit his daughter Emily, who was married and living at Hazel Run. While there, he fell very ill. He knew that Mexicans were waiting for him in Natchitoches, Louisiana, and asked Stephen to meet them in his place and take over for him until he was well again.

Stephen left New Orleans on the steamboat *Beaver* with eight or ten men who were interested in the Texas venture. In Natchitoches he met Don Erasmo Seguin and several other Spaniards, who were waiting to escort his father on a trip to explore Texas and select the land for his colony. They greeted Stephen with great friendliness, entertained him at dinners, and gave a ball in his honor.

When they had completed plans for the trip, Stephen took his father's tomahawk and wilderness pack and started out with them. But after only a few days he received news of his father's death.

"He called me to his bedside," the letter from his mother said, "and with much distress and difficulty of speech begged me to tell you to take his place, and if God in his wisdom thought best to disappoint him in the accomplishment of his wishes and plans formed for the benefit of his family, he prayed him to extend his goodness to you and enable you to go on with the business in the same way he would have done had not sickness and . . . death prevented him."

All that day and the next, as Stephen and his party returned to Natchitoches, he thought about his father's last request.

The sting of tears was in his eyes and the ache of tears in his throat. His heart was heavy with grief for his father and burdened, too, with the choice he must make.

In New Orleans, he would have success in a profession that he liked better each day of his studies. He would have the pleasant life of a city, filled with friendships.

In Texas, he would have hard work and the risk of failure, and the crude, lonely life of the frontier.

But he thought of his father's desperate struggle to carry out what he considered the greatest and best plan of his life, of his dying request to his son.

There was only one answer Stephen could make.

The night they returned to Natchitoches he sat down by a flickering candle and wrote to his mother.

"My dear Mother and Sister," he said, "I have just heard the melancholy news of the death of my father. His exertions on the trip to San Antonio and after his return were too much. He suffered more than you or anyone else can imagine who has not seen this wild country. . . . This news has affected me very much. He was one of the most feeling and affectionate fathers that ever lived. . . .

"This most unhappy event will not retard the progress of settlement. I shall go out and take possession of the land and arrange for the families to move in the fall — so that I still hope great good will result from my father's astonishing perseverance and fatigue last winter. . . .

"Farewell, my Dear Mother. May heaven preserve you once more to meet your affectionate son

S F Austin"

6:

Into the Wilderness

Two days later Austin set out to join Don Erasmo Seguin and the rest of the exploring party again. Next day he met them, and they continued to ride deeper into Texas.

Austin was sad, both because of his father's death and because of the sacrifice of his own plans. But before many days he became enthusiastic about Texas.

It was not that the trip through the wilderness was a new and exciting adventure for him. He had lived most of his life on the frontier, and he had traveled through wildernesses from Missouri to Connecticut, from Connecticut to Kentucky, from Arkansas to Louisiana. But this country was different.

"The grass is more abundant and of a ranker and more luxurious growth than I have ever seen before in any country," he wrote in his journal on July 20.

On August 10, he wrote, "Came on to the Guadalupe River. Country the most beautiful I ever saw — rolling prairies — soil very black and deep. . . . The Guadalupe is a beautiful bold stream of perfectly clear limestone water, banks very high."

On September 4, he wrote, "Came on to Guadalupe River 12 miles. Prairie gently rolling and generally good, wide bottoms, heavy timber of oak, pecan, etc.

"Deer being plenty, some of the party went ahunting and some fishing. The hunters brought in a fat buck, and the fishermen two fine soft-shelled turtles and one fish. The turtles were very fat and made good soup with no other seasoning than salt and pepper."

"Deer and mustang horses very plenty," he continued in his journal next day. "Saw at least 400 of the former and 150 of the latter. One mustang colt got separated from the gang, came on with us. . . . Alligators plenty."

On August 12, when Austin's party neared San Antonio, messengers from there rode out to meet them. They brought food prepared by the wives of those of the party who lived in San Antonio, and had exciting news — news that the Mexicans greeted with joyous cries of "Viva Independencia."

Austin joined in their feasting and rejoicing, never dreaming that the news that made them so happy would a few months later bring trouble for him.

It was the news that Mexico had won its independence from Spain.

After a few days in San Antonio, the little party of explorers were on their way again. Altogether they traveled for almost three months, and in all that time came to only two towns. One was San Antonio, the other Goliad, generally called La Bahia. Both were sites of missions, and both had garrisons of soldiers, but San Antonio was the larger. Both were of a type new to Austin, with their low, flat-roofed adobe houses built right up to the dusty, straggling streets. In spite of the poor way most of the people there lived, the little villages with their trees and flowers and unhurried, courteous people were very charming.

There were sixteen in Austin's party, and almost the only

people they met were Indians. When they had been traveling a few days, a man going the opposite way told them of having seen three corpses on the road, the victims of Indians.

The rest of the day they rode warily, and when they camped for the night, they decided to take turn as guards. The first part of the night passed quietly, but when Dr. Hewitson was on guard between two and three o'clock, he saw something suspicious and alarmed the camp.

"Wake up," he said in a low, tense tone, going to each one and shaking him. "I just saw several Indians prowling over there."

Quickly the men grabbed their guns. They formed a tight circle about their dead camp fire and peered into the darkness.

"There!" whispered the doctor excitedly. "There they are! Riding on white horses!"

"Yes," agreed Beard. "I see them, too. Let's shoot them before they get us."

"No," Austin ordered quickly. "Hold your fire. I don't see anything. But if I did, I'd still say not to shoot. As sure as we fire a gun, they will attack. If we don't shoot, maybe they will pass us by."

The men argued under their breath but obeyed.

"I see them," insisted the doctor. "Look! Don't you see those white horses? When the wind blows the weeds and branches, you can see them plain."

"I see them," another agreed. "Looks like they're just sitting on their horses, waiting."

"Well, we can wait as long as they can," Austin said firmly. "Let's try to get some rest."

But no one could sleep. They sat or stood with their guns at hand, staring into the black shadows, stiffening at every small night noise. But no attack came.

When it was light enough to see, Austin walked over to the place where the Indians had been seen. Suddenly he gave a shout of laughter. "Come here, Doctor," he called. "Take a good look at your Indians on white horses."

The men hurried over. There they saw a tree stump whitened by sun and rain and the white roots of some fallen trees.

"There are your Indians on white horses," Austin said, as the men joined in his laughter. "That's what we lost sleep over — some very fierce tree stumps!"

Twice they met real Indians, and several times they heard reports of recent Indian attacks.

One evening after they had made camp, about twenty Indians came up to them, four chiefs, ten squaws, and several young braves. Since their manner was peaceful, Austin's party met them with friendliness. One of the chiefs was Gocosa, the head chief of the Tonkawa Indians. Austin gave him some tobacco and smoked with him.

Through an interpreter, they had a long talk. Austin told about his explorations and about the settlement he planned.

Gocosa was pleased and helpful. Next day he sent two of his sons to guide Austin to their village, where he was treated with great courtesy.

About a month later Austin's party was alarmed by a war whoop. The little group quickly gathered to defend themselves and stood in silence but with their guns ready. A chief and a dozen braves came up, followed by some boys and five squaws.

The chief walked over to Austin. "We are friendly," he said in Spanish.

"Our friends are welcome," Austin replied.

"Tobacco for friends?" the chief asked.

Austin gave him some tobacco.

"Smoke with friends?" the chief invited.

"No," Austin decided. "We have no time to sit and smoke. We must go on with our explorations. But here is plenty of tobacco for you and your braves."

The chief was not satisfied. He and his warriors followed Austin's party, begging for this and that. Finally Austin gave them an old frying pan. The Indians all stopped to examine it.

Austin and his men continued their journey, glad to be rid of their begging "friends."

As they rode across the land, Austin began to love it. In the cool quiet of early dawn, dewdrops hung like softly gleaming pearls along the spiderwebs that stretched from weed to weed, and when the sun rose, the whole countryside sparkled. He rode through grass so tall it reached above his stirrups, and sunflowers and tall yellow daisies bloomed in huge patches. Birds and wild turkeys, squirrels and rabbits, herds of deer and wild cattle and horses abounded on the prairies.

After the heat of the day, the water from the quiet green rivers and clear rippling creeks was cool and delicious. And at night when he lay with his hands under his head and looked up at the stars, bigger and brighter than any he had seen before, he would think about the riches and beauty of this land.

And when the summer moon rose, big and golden, and mockingbirds filled the night with sweet melodies, a dream began to grow in him.

He thought of the poor people he had seen, hungry, ragged, living miserably. He thought of the hard times then in the United States, when willing workers could find no jobs, when men were losing their homes and farms and businesses and were facing a life without hope.

Here was a place where they could begin anew, a rich land ready to yield its riches in bountiful crops. And a free land for the settler who was strong enough and brave enough to work for it. Great good might indeed come of his father's plans.

When he had completed his explorations, Austin returned to Natchitoches. There he made his request to the Mexican government for the land he had selected. He had chosen the land that lay between the Colorado and the Brazos rivers as being the best located and most fertile.

Then he went to New Orleans to make final arrangements with families who wanted to join his colony.

He needed money to get the colony started and tried to interest Mr. Hawkins, the friend in whose office he had studied law.

"Well, I'll have to think it over," said Mr. Hawkins. "Your description of the country sounds most interesting. Tell me more about your plans. Just what are you trying to do?"

"I am trying to settle three hundred families on the land that the Mexican government has granted to me in Texas."

"Do you own this land?"

"Oh, no. The government will give me a certain number of acres for every family I settle there. That will be the only land I shall own."

"Are you selling the land in the grant to the settlers?"

"No, it will be given to them. They will become the owners by living on it, farming or running businesses in the towns."

"But surely the land will not be entirely free."

"No," Austin replied again, "but almost. I intend to charge twelve and a half cents an acre for my work in getting the land for them. You see, I secured the grant from the Mexican government. With this permission, settlers from the United States will be allowed to move to Texas on the land I have selected, but no other settlers will be admitted."

"Twelve and a half cents an acre is certainly cheap enough. Government land in the United States costs ten times that much."

"Yes," Austin continued. "And besides getting permission for the settlers to come to Texas, I shall survey their land for them and give them a good deed to it, all for the same fee."

"That seems reasonable enough. How much land will each settler get?"

"That will depend on the size of his family and his ability to farm or start a business. Each married man will get six hundred and forty acres for himself, three hundred and twenty acres for his wife, one hundred and sixty acres for each child, and eighty acres for each slave. Town lots will be given to blacksmiths, merchants, doctors, and the like."

"That seems to be a very attractive proposition. Very attractive indeed. Especially if the land is as good as you say."

"It is."

"Without doubt a great many people will want to join your colony, especially the lazy and the lawless who will see a chance for big profit with little work."

"There will be big profit. Of that I am sure. But there will not be little work. Texas is a wilderness, and it will take great work to build farms and cities there. I shall make that clear. Besides, I shall select only the best type of settler. The Mexican government demands that each become a member of the Roman Catholic Church and a citizen of Mexico. And I shall demand a certificate showing each settler's Christian morality and general character. Only men of integrity, sobriety, and industry will be accepted for my colony."

"That will be fine if you can enforce it."

"I can enforce it," Austin said with quiet confidence. "I have so many requests already that I know I can choose only the highest type of settler."

He rose suddenly and walked over to the desk. "Mr. Hawkins," he exclaimed, "you ought to see the Texas land. Grass up to your stirrups, crystal clear water, timber in abundance. It's like nothing I've ever seen before. A man can make a fortune there, a fortune!"

Hawkins was convinced and agreed to lend Austin the money he needed. With this help Austin bought tools and provisions necessary to start his colony and a small ship, the *Lively*, to take settlers to Texas across the Gulf of Mexico instead of by the long, hard overland route.

7:

Texas Colony

THE *Lively* set sail with provisions, tools and seed, and about twenty settlers, but Austin joined a group of settlers traveling by land.

This group of colonists traveled in a wagon caravan. They crossed the Brazos and entered Austin's grant December 31, 1821. On New Year's Day they pitched camp and started selecting their land near a little creek which they named New Year's Creek.

As soon as a family chose the land for their home, the men began felling trees and cutting them into logs for the cabins. The women bustled about cooking a big New Year's dinner, and the children helped their parents when called upon and then as soon as possible slipped off to explore the creek and woods like eager young puppies. Everywhere there was laughter and shouting and a great happy helpfulness.

Austin took his tomahawk, the one his father had carried on his first trip to Texas, and helped the men clear out the under-brush.

His heart beat high with the thought that now his colony had actually begun. He knew how happy his father would have been at this moment. And his mind was full of dreams of how this little beginning would grow to a great fulfillment, bringing good to thousands of people then unborn.

The time of growth would not be easy. There would be danger and hardship enough: Indian troubles, drought and flood, crop failure and disease, impatience and disunity. But Austin believed that his colonists were sturdy and brave and good, and he felt that he was strong enough to guide them to success.

When they had finished their New Year's feast, Austin rose and made a little speech.

"The sound of the ax ringing in this wilderness is music to my ears," he said. "My ambition is to redeem this fine country — our glorious Texas — and make it a home for the unfortunate, a refuge from poverty. To succeed in redeeming Texas from its wilderness state by means of the plough alone. . . .

"I wish Texas to be improved by the introduction of in-dustrious and agricultural citizens. I want the savage Indians subdued; the frontier protected; the lands cultivated; roads and canals opened; river navigation developed and the rivers covered with boats and barges carrying to the coast the produce of the interior for export in exchange for foreign products. I wish to take from my native country and every other land the best that they contain and plant it in my adopted country — that is, their best inhabitants, their industry, and their enlightenment.

"These are the magnificent plans I have for Texas.

"These, my friends, are the plans I share with you. For my ambition is to build up for the present as well as for future generations.

"And with God's blessing and help, may this be the beginning of a life for each of you as free and liberal as any man could wish, with peace and happiness, with Bread in abundance, and contentment in every heart."

Next day Austin left these colonists and traveled to the mouth of the Colorado, where his ship, the *Lively,* was to land. But he waited for it in vain. By mistake it had landed its passengers at the Brazos instead of the Colorado, and sailed away. The settlers wandered about looking for Austin, but most of them became discouraged and found their way back to the United States.

But Austin did not know this. He waited for the *Lively* until March and then gave these settlers up as lost. Greatly disappointed, he returned to San Antonio, where he heard more bad news — bad news which had been brewing for him since the day when he had cheered the news of Mexican independence with his friends.

For now he learned that the new government in Mexico

did not recognize his right as a colonizer. It did not recognize him in his father's place.

This meant that all the settlers who had left the United States and moved to Texas were really without the right to be there. They were really homeless.

To prevent the loss of everything they had planned, to prevent the hardship and suffering they must endure if their claims were not allowed, there was only one thing that Austin could do. He must go to Mexico City and persuade the government to recognize his contracts as legal and binding.

It would be a long journey of twelve hundred miles, and a dangerous one through a wilderness inhabited by savage Indians, on roads infested with thieves and bandits. It would be an expensive journey, too, and Austin had little money. But he did not hesitate.

He appointed Josiah H. Bell to take his place with the colonists until his return, arranged for his brother Brown to stay with friends in San Antonio, got a passport from Governor Martinez at San Antonio on March 13, and set out for Mexico City.

The first part of the journey he traveled with two men who were going in the same direction, Dr. Robert Andrews and Mr. Waters.

They rode without incident for several days. Then, early one morning, Austin woke with a bad headache.

"I must have coffee before I can start another day in the saddle," he said.

"Better not risk a fire," Dr. Andrews warned. "If there are

Indians around, they'll see the smoke and attack."

"This is Indian country, you know," Waters added.

Austin looked at the countryside. As far as he could see — and the land was not hilly — there was no one. It seemed impossible that Indians could be lurking in any of the little thickets, and the rest of the land was prairie covered with tall grass. He felt so ill that he decided to build the fire and make coffee.

To keep it hidden as much as possible, he found a small gully and climbed down and built his fire there, while Dr. Andrews and Waters went after the horses. As was usual, the horses had been hobbled by tying their front feet together and were grazing somewhere near.

Austin built only a little fire, but its smoke rose straight and white in the still morning air. Soon his coffee was boiling and he stamped the fire out and smothered it with sand. But as he was pouring his coffee, he heard the noise of hoofbeats.

He jumped up and climbed out of the gully and saw a band of Comanches racing toward him. They were led by two Indian girls blowing trumpets, and the spears they carried glittered in the early sunlight.

Austin grabbed his gun, but he knew that it was of no use to him against so many warriors on horseback. He went over and stood on his saddlebags, which held his money and important papers, and waited.

The warriors thundered up, and when they came near, their columns divided, one going to the right, the other to the left, so that in an instant he was encircled by a ring of Indians.

Shouting, they jumped down and began plundering the camp, snatching blankets, coffeepot, food, and saddles. They pushed Austin off the saddlebags and carried them away with cries of satisfaction. Several Indians caught Waters and Dr. Andrews and brought them back to the camp. But they did not attempt to kill their captives.

All the Indians were whooping and yelling, and Austin was surprised to hear Waters and Dr. Andrews shouting too. "Americans," they were shouting. "We are not Mexicans! We are Americans!"

Over and over they repeated their cry, until at last they caught the interest of the Comanches.

Suddenly Austin remembered being told that though the Indians hated Mexicans, they were generally friendly to Americans.

When the Indians quieted to listen to Andrews and Waters, Austin firmly twisted himself free from the Indian who held him and walked up to the Comanche chief. "I am an American," he said. Spear in hand, the chief listened but said nothing.

"Is your nation at war with my nation?" Austin asked, using his few words of Spanish.

The chief understood him. "No," he answered.

"Do you like Americans?"

"Yes, they are our friends."

"Where do you get your spearheads?"

"From the Americans."

"Where do you get guns?"

"From the Americans."

"Where do you get blankets?"

"From the Americans."

"Where do you trade your horses and pelts?"

"To our good friends the Americans."

"Well, do you think that if you were passing through their nation, as I am passing through yours, they would rob you as you have robbed me?"

The chief thought a minute. Then, "No," he said. "It would not be right."

He turned and ordered his warriors to give back the stolen articles. Slowly, reluctantly, without a word, the Comanches piled everything in a heap and mounted their horses.

But Austin noticed that his saddlebags were not returned. He asked for them and looked everywhere but could not find them. Then he saw that one of the squaws was having trouble with her mustang. She beat and kicked it, but it balked and would not leave.

"There must be a reason for the horse's stubbornness," Austin thought swiftly and ran over to the squaw. He was right, for the blanket on the horse had a queer bulge. Austin jerked it up, and there were the missing saddlebags. He pulled them out as the warriors laughed at the embarrassed squaw. Angry and ashamed, she kicked her mustang again, and this time it trotted off.

The chief gave a command, and the whole circle of warriors raced away as quickly as they had come.

The three men, feeling lucky to have escaped so lightly, sorted their belongings and loaded the pack mule again. The Indians had returned almost everything. One thing they had kept was a Spanish grammar. Austin had tied it to his saddle horn so that he could study Spanish as he rode along, for he knew he would need to speak Spanish.

Much later, when Austin was in Mexico, some traders found this grammar in an Indian camp. Seeing the name Stephen F. Austin in the book, they thought that Austin had been killed by the Comanches and spread the word that he was dead.

This false report reached his colonists, who were much discouraged by the news. It even went to his mother and sister in far-off Missouri and brought them months of grief before they learned that Austin was still alive.

Waters and Dr. Andrews traveled with Austin as far as Laredo, on the Rio Grande. Then from Laredo to Monterey he traveled with a group of people, for the road was not safe for a lone traveler. He reached Monterey on April 10, having been on the road for almost a month.

From Monterey he traveled with only one man. The road was a dangerous one, with bandits lying in wait for rich travelers or pack trains. To protect themselves, Austin and his companion traded their clothes for ragged ones. Over these rags each wore a torn, dirty blanket of the kind the Mexicans called serapes. Austin hid his money and important papers in his boots.

In this disguise, with his dark brown hair and sun-tanned skin, Austin passed readily as a poor Mexican soldier going to Mexico City to ask for a pension.

Austin and his fellow-traveler enjoyed this game of masquerade. Austin liked the fun of outwitting men who would very likely have cut his throat if they had known he had four hundred dollars in his boots. But several times he was brought face to face with the fact that he was playing a game with his life at stake, and he would gladly have given the excitement for a safe, quiet road.

It took them nineteen days to travel from Monterey to

Mexico City. As they neared the end of the journey, Austin spent much time planning how he could get the Mexican government to approve the grant for his colony. But when he thought of the difficulties of his task, his heart began to fail him.

The road twisted like a snake up and up around the mountains. At the crest Austin paused to gaze at the magnificent view, while his companion began the long descent.

Grandeur was all about him, as far as he could see. Near at hand the mountains were strong and rugged, gray and bare or bristling with green growth. But afar they looked soft as a crumpled length of silk, like changeable taffeta, blue and purple. And far below they were veiled with the misty white of clouds.

For a long time Austin stood there, feeling rather than thinking. The hugeness and the vastness of the mountains made him feel very small and unimportant.

What could he hope to accomplish in Mexico City? How could he, one man alone, change the decision of a government? He, a stranger without a single friend in the city, an unwelcome foreigner who did not even know the Spanish language well?

Gradually the peace and strength around him comforted him.

He remembered the colonists who had depended on his contract and would be homeless if it were not recognized. His cause was right and just.

Man might be small, but right and justice were majestic as the mountains. And man working for right and justice became strong too.

8:

To Mexico City

AUSTIN entered Mexico City still in his disguise and wandered about unnoticed in the throng of people as poorly dressed as he. At last he came to the square in the heart of the city.

Mexico's great and beautiful cathedral with its twin towers and lovely ornamented walls faced this plaza, as did the government building where Austin would spend his days. This was a handsome block-long building of two stories, called the Palace.

"This city is truly a magnificent one," Austin thought, "larger than New York and with much more beautiful buildings."

He was pleasantly excited by the splendid buildings and crowds of people and eager to get on with his work. But first he must dress properly.

He was glad that his father had taught him the importance of being dressed suitably. For the Mexicans, too, set great store upon proper dress. They would expect a man asking for two hundred thousand acres of Mexican land to look like an important person. To appear before them carelessly dressed would be to insult them. And so Austin spent some of his four hundred dollars on a suitable outfit.

When, clean and shaven and dressed in his new clothes, Austin looked into the mirror, he gave himself a reassuring smile. It was a handsome young man that smiled back at him, dressed in quiet elegance from his hat, frilled white shirt, and white gloves to his shining black boots. There was a twinkle in his eyes as he inspected himself. Perhaps all this finery was nearly as much a disguise as the rags he had just taken off!

But he looked like what he wanted the Mexicans to think him, a confident and successful young man whom they could be proud to claim as their representative in Texas.

The officials received him courteously; yet there was a great delay. Austin expected to finish his business within a few days, but it was two weeks before he could even present to Congress his request to have his contract recognized. Then, just as it seemed Congress might grant his request, the Mexicans overthrew their new government and chose General Iturbide as their emperor.

Austin told about this event in a letter to his brother, who had decided to join him in the Texas venture and was waiting for him in San Antonio.

"Firing of musketry and cannon in the air loaded with Balls, and loud shouts from the soldiers and citizens proclaimed Iturbide emperor. . . . This day has been a constant scene of rejoicing, the Army paraded and the Bells have kept a constant roar since daylight. I hope this event will be a fortunate one for the country."

It was not a fortunate one for Austin. In the confusion of reorganizing the government, Congress had no time for him. Austin realized that it might be months before he could leave.

Disappointed as he was, he taught himself to accept the delay with patience and filled his days with activities to keep from fretting about the condition of his colonists.

Much of his time went to keeping his contract in the thoughts of congressmen. He used every opportunity to persuade them to recognize his claim, just short of becoming a nuisance. Besides writing letters to be read in Congress, he made the acquaintance of every member of Congress and explained the situation to each one. Many of these men became his friends.

"What I am asking is not alone for my benefit or for the good of the Texas settlers," he explained. "It has many advantages for Mexico too. My colonists will build productive farms and prosperous towns. This will undoubtedly increase the value of Texas, which is now mere wilderness, and thus add greatly to the wealth of Mexico. Furthermore, the colony will help the Mexican officials in Texas to solve one of their worst problems, their trouble with the Indians. My colonists are brave and self-reliant men. They will organize to protect their homes and will punish Indians who attack them. Soon you will find your Indian problem solved."

His new acquaintances listened courteously, and many agreed with him. But still they did not act on his request. For one thing, they were working on a new constitution for their country. Mexico was now Austin's country, too, and he gave his new countrymen the advantage of his knowledge of the Constitution of the United States and the American system of government. He wrote out sample constitutions, which he gave to his friends, and in influencing their thinking, he indirectly helped to write the constitution that Mexico finally adopted.

But Austin could not spend all his time working either for his own cause or for his adopted country. One other thing that helped to keep him busy was studying Spanish. He bought another grammar to replace the one stolen by the Indians and spent much of siesta time, when life in Mexico stopped for an afternoon rest, studying Spanish.

He progressed so rapidly that in three months he was writing his own Spanish letters to Congress. And the better he spoke and wrote Spanish, the more welcome he was as a guest in Mexican homes.

Austin received many invitations, for as a man seeking to become a colonizer of Texas, an *empresario,* he was an important person. At first Mexican congressmen and government officials invited him to their homes as a matter of formal courtesy, but when they learned to know him, they repeated their invitations because they liked him.

They considered most Americans crude and ill-mannered, boastful of themselves and scornful of others. But Austin was different. He respected and practiced their ceremonious good manners. He tried to understand their way of life and was interested in their land and customs. And so once again Austin's friendliness and amiability won him new friends.

Austin enjoyed the hospitality extended to him. He liked the good talk after his months of talking to only a few people in the wilderness, the lively banter of the social gatherings and the satisfying talk about government and politics. He liked the music and color of the fiestas, the elegance of the dances, and the glamorous make-believe of the opera and theater.

Sometimes he felt a little guilty about his pleasure when he thought of his colonists struggling in lonely Texas. But he was doing everything he could for them. Common sense told him it was best to be as patient and happy as he could.

Besides his companionship with his new friends, there were two other things Austin especially enjoyed in Mexico. One was the plants, the other, history. In the patios of the homes where he visited and in the beautiful public parks he found many lovely flowers, vines, and shrubs that he had never seen before. He was fascinated by the ancient twisted cypress trees, already old when Columbus discovered America. He collected seeds of his favorite plants to take back to Texas.

History was Austin's favorite reading matter, and in Mexico City, so much older than any city in the United States, he felt himself surrounded by history. Such things as the graceful arches of the aqueducts, the huge stone Calendar, and the mysterious Pyramid of the Sun not far from the city set him to asking questions, and he listened eagerly to facts and legends about Mexico's ancient Aztec civilization and Cortez, its conqueror.

But not everything he saw in Mexico City pleased him. "A great proportion of the people are most miserably poor and wretched," he wrote his brother. "Beggars are more numerous than I ever saw in any place in my life — robberies are frequent in the streets — the people are bigoted and superstitious to an extreme, and indolence seems to be the order of the day."

Eight months passed slowly, and at last it seemed that Congress was ready to act on Austin's case. Then, on December 2, Santa Anna led a revolt to overthrow the government again. Emperor Iturbide successfully crushed this rebellion, and there was a great celebration when he returned to Mexico City.

The street from the triumphal arch to the Palace was decorated with bright-colored fringed paper festoons and lit by lamps hung from the festoons to look like millions of tiny stars. At the entrance to the Palace and on the plaza were splendid life-size images of the Virgin Mary clothed in silver. There was a constant display of fireworks and a constant pealing of bells, and the crowd was so great that there was scarcely room for the parade to move.

The procession was led by friars and priests carrying crosses. Then came a gilt car with a large portrait of the Emperor, followed by the Emperor's bodyguard of seventy-five handsome horsemen. Next came a band playing spirited music.

A detachment of infantry completed the parade.

Austin shared the excitement of the huge crowd, the feeling of being present at a history-making event, but he hoped that now at last Congress would pass a colonization law and he could go home.

He was growing more worried about his colony every day, more afraid that it would fall apart before he could get back to it. He wrote letters to the leaders in the colony explaining his long absence, but he felt that it was only natural that they should lose faith in him after so long a time.

He was worried about money, too. The four hundred dollars he had started out with had long since been spent, as had more money sent by Mr. Hawkins from New Orleans and more

that he had borrowed in Mexico. He had even sold his watch for one hundred dollars. He lived as carefully as he could, but his position demanded that he live well.

The Christmas season came, and in spite of his worry, Austin took pleasure in the Christmas customs of Mexico. He heard of the *posada,* which was really a series of parties. Each night the week before Christmas, the group would gather and knock at the door of one of the members, asking, as did Mary and Joseph in Bethlehem, for a place to stay. Each night they would be turned away until Christmas Eve, when they would be welcomed. But each night after the ceremony of the pilgrimage there would be a party with feasting and merriment.

For the first time he heard of *Los Pastores,* a quaint and

reverent pageant of the Nativity. He learned, too, that instead of looking under a Christmas tree for their presents, or hanging up their stockings, Mexican children broke a *piñata*. A *piñata* was a large, gayly decorated clay jar filled with candy and little gifts. Blindfolded children took turns trying to break the *piñata*, shouting with laughter when the gifts came tumbling down.

But interesting as these customs were, seeing the happiness of his friends made Austin homesick for his own family. His loneliness and disappointment showed in a letter he wrote on New Year's Day, 1823, just a year after the arrival of his colonists in Texas.

"I remember that the last time our unfortunate family were all united was four years ago this day in Herculaneum. It was the last time we were permitted to assemble under the paternal roof. Since then how many troubles and fatigues have we all experienced! I trust that it will not be much longer before we shall be once more living under the same roof."

But it was not until February that Congress finally passed the decree Austin had been waiting for. His colony was approved; all he needed was for the officers to sign the decree and he could leave for Texas.

But days dragged on without the decree's being signed.

On March 10, Austin made another plea. Very politely he told of the sad condition of his waiting colony and said that if only the decree were signed he could return to Texas with a group of travelers going north in a few days.

Wonder of wonders, His Excellency signed the decree!

But before the travelers left, the government was overthrown once again. The new Congress immediately declared all acts of the old Congress null and void. Austin was right back where he had started.

It was a heart-breaking disappointment for Austin, but he accepted it calmly. Quietly but firmly he at once submitted a new application to Congress. Again he went to all his friends and urged them to vote for his colony, and this time he was successful. His colony was finally approved on April 14, a year and a month from the time he had left San Antonio.

It had been a long, lonesome, discouraging time, but Austin returned to Texas with more than he had originally asked for. Instead of three hundred families he could settle six hundred. Instead of six hundred forty acres for each man he could give four thousand six hundred acres.

He came back with two titles, *empresario,* meaning colonizer, and colonel. As *empresario* he would bring in colonists, issue their land titles, help them start their new life, make needed laws, and enforce these laws. As colonel he would organize and head the militia, the soldiers needed for the protection of the colony from Indians and law-breakers.

Besides winning the full approval of his colonization Austin won the respect and admiration of many influential Mexicans. In public statements they praised him for his "energy, patience, and perseverance" and "for his personal qualities and for the desires which animated him to be useful in the empire."

9:

Indian Trouble

AUSTIN returned to Texas with the presents his brother had asked for, a Mexican saddle and a wide-brimmed white wool hat. After a happy reunion with Brown and long talks with his friends in San Antonio, he was eager to begin surveying the land and forming the government of his colony. He was delighted to learn that there were more settlers now than when he had left for Mexico.

He began by visiting as many of the colonists as he could, taking them the good news that their titles were safe and that they would have more than five times as much land as they had expected. They needed good news, for their first year had been hard. No one had made a crop, because of a bad drought, and almost the only food was fish and wild game. Most of the meat was mustang meat, since these wild horses were plentiful and easy to hunt.

Only about twenty of the original forty-five families had stayed, but new settlers had arrived. Austin found most of them busy and cheerful in spite of their hardships. Even those who were discouraged caught his enthusiasm and began making big plans for the colony. After he had gone, the man of the family would plow a piece of land for a second planting of corn, or cut stakes for a fence to protect his young cotton from being trampled by deer or mustangs. And the woman of the house would get out the calico she had been saving and decide to use it for curtains, or begin planning to add a lean-to to the cabin.

But everywhere Austin went, the settlers complained about the Indians.

"Those pesky Redskins sneaked the washing right off my clothesline," one woman would grumble.

"They stole my milk cow, my only milk cow," another would add, "and my pigs, and my whole store of corn."

"The Wacos got off with all my horses," one man reported. "I can show you the pen they made in the woods to trap them."

One morning Austin learned with anger that some Tonkawas had been bold enough to steal his own horses, the entire string.

The Indians didn't always stop with robbery. They terrorized the colonists in many other ways, sometimes even killing settlers who fought back.

One tribe decided which families to let alone and which to

terrorize by sending a young boy of the tribe to the cabin, alone and pretending to need help. If the family fed this boy and treated him kindly, they were safe from these Indians. But if they were cruel or unkind, they were repaid by Indian thievery or attacks.

The Rabb family had such trying experiences with the Waco Indians that they decided to move to a safer neighborhood. Their wagon was loaded and they were just driving up the last of their pigs when they saw about thirty Indians riding toward them. Just then the hogs broke away, and their friend Ingram went after them. The Rabbs quickly unloaded the wagon and barricaded themselves in the cabin. By the time Ingram returned there were almost two hundred warriors circling the cabin, uttering war whoops and demanding corn.

Ingram pretended to go after corn for them, but really he went to get help. The nearest neighbor was twelve miles away. There he found three men who rode back with him.

It was night by the time they neared the Rabb place. They saw the red glow of fire in the sky and heard spine-tingling war whoops and dreaded the sight of death and destruction ahead of them. But when they crept close enough, they saw that the glow came from a circle of camp fires that surrounded the cabin. Occasionally the Indians would throw burning torches into the darkness to reveal anyone who was trying to sneak up, but Ingram and the other three men managed to return to their horses unseen.

Then they rode boldly up to the chief. He asked them if

any more Americans were coming. Ingram told him firmly many more. The old chief spoke to his warriors, and the rest of the night they were quiet. Next morning they rode away.

Not all the settlers were lucky enough to escape with no more than a bad fright. Austin found that he could not even get surveying parties to go out, because of Indian raids against them. He decided that his first duty was to make his colony safe from the Indians.

There were three main tribes of Indians harassing Austin's colony — the Wacos, the Tonkawas, and the Karankawas. Along the coast, where settlers arriving by boat must land, lived the most savage of the Indians, the Karankawas, who were believed to be cannibals.

They were very large and strong, some warriors being almost seven feet tall. They never wore moccasins, and the prints of their big, bare feet in the moist sand looked like the tracks of some huge beast. The men braided their hair with bits of cloth and tied rattlesnake rattlers at the end of the braids. The girls wore knee-length skirts of fringed leather. On the fringe they tied beads, shells, and bits of glass, so that a tinkling sound was made as they walked.

They lived mostly on fish and alligators. They kept no domestic animals except dogs, and never rode horses. They were excellent swimmers and very skillful in handling canoes, and they were fierce hunters. Each warrior had a bow as tall as he, so strong and powerful that an average man could not even shoot it. The Karankawa hunter shot his arrows with such terrific speed that he could kill large animals at a great distance.

The colonists who came by way of the Gulf of Mexico had to pass through Karankawa country. They had to run the danger of having their goods stolen by the Indians and their guards murdered.

These Karankawas were so hated and feared by the colonists that one of Austin's first expeditions was against them. In 1824 he himself led a band of sixty Texans in an effort to subdue them. For weeks the Texans wandered through the wilderness looking for the Karankawas, but the Indians kept out of sight. Finally Austin and his men had to go home for more supplies. After a short rest they set out again, this time with ninety men. They soon found the Indians, who tried to outwit the Texans by fleeing to the protection of the priests at the old Spanish mission at La Bahia. The Indians thought they would be safe there, for the Texans would not attack a mission.

But Austin threatened that unless they sent representatives to talk peace with him, he would attack. Several priests and men of the town came out and met with Austin. They made an agreement that the Karankawas should stay in their own hunting grounds and not come into Austin's colony. Realizing that Austin meant it when he said that the Texans would punish them if they broke this treaty, the Indians kept it fairly well.

On another occasion, Austin had led an expedition against the Tonkawas, who had stolen a string of horses. He met with their chief, Carita, and insisted that the horses should be returned and the thieves publicly whipped. Such a punishment was con-

sidered very shameful by the Indians. Most of them would rather be killed than whipped.

After the public whipping, the Tonkawas were not so much of a danger to the colonists, though it was not until eight months later that Carita finally signed a treaty with Austin.

Austin tried to persuade the Tonkawas to settle down and farm. He taught Carita how to plant corn and gave him hoes and a good supply of seed corn. Carita promised that his men would clear land in the Brazos River bottom and grow their own corn instead of begging or stealing it.

But in a few months he was back asking for more corn.

"What about your own crop of corn?" Austin asked.

"We did not make a crop," Carita replied.

"Why not? The season was good for corn."

"We did not plant the corn you gave us. We ground it and used it for bread."

"You promised to plant it. Why didn't you keep your promise?" Austin demanded sternly.

"Carita was inspired by the Great Spirit," the chief explained piously, posing with one arm raised high. "In a vision the Great Spirit spoke to Carita. 'The Tonkawas must not grow corn,' the Great Spirit said. 'They must hunt as they have always done, and look to their white friends for corn for their bread.' And so we obey the Great Spirit. We have come to our white friends for bread."

Austin raised his hand in the same pose Carita had taken. "I too have had a vision," he said. "The Great Spirit instructs me to say that if the Tonkawas do not go to work, they will starve."

In June, 1824, news came that the Waco Indians had killed a settler named Tomlinson, and Austin sent an expedition against them. He did not lead the force himself but sent a group of trusted men with his message and a supply of tobacco, cloth, and trinkets to barter for horses and mules.

On a quiet summer day, the band of Texans topped a gentle hill and looked down on the Waco village. It was a pleasant, peaceful sight. The Wacos lived in cone-shaped lodges made of cedar logs, thatched with grass. These lodges were grouped around their council house, which was similar but much larger, fifty-nine paces in circumference. On the outskirts of the village were small fields of corn, beans, melons, and pumpkins.

The Indians were in a peaceful mood, for they had just returned from a successful summer buffalo hunt and were feasting on buffalo meat, beans, and green corn. They invited the Texans to their council house and smoked the pipe of peace with them. The leader of the Texans read Austin's message.

"I call you brothers," Austin wrote, "because the chiefs of your nation who came to the Colorado about three moons ago told the Americans who live there that the Wacos and Tawakanes were friends and wished to be at peace with them. . . .

"The Americans will be at peace with the Wacos and Tawakanes and trade with them as friends and brothers provided that the chiefs of that nation will agree to punish the murder of Tomlinson. The path between us will be clean, and both parties can travel in safety. The Wacos and Tawakanes must not disturb the settlers on the Brazos or Colorado, and if any of those settlers misuse any of your nation, I will punish them for it if the chief will inform me, and if any of your nation steal from or misuse any of the Americans the chief must deliver them to the Americans to be killed or whipped according to the crime they have committed. In this way we may keep a peace between us as long as the sun shall shine. All the bad men will then be punished and all the good ones can live in their houses and villages with the women and children and plant their corn in peace and safety. My friends the Americans are a great people; they are like the leaves on the trees; they are all good warriors — and well armed. They are true friends and dangerous enemies. They never beg peace of any nation. They are always ready for war or peace but they prefer peace, for they wish to be friends and brothers of all the Indians of this province. The Wacos and Tawakanes can therefore choose and send me word by the young men whether they are willing to punish the murder of Tomlinson and be at peace with the Americans or whether they wish for war."

The Indians agreed to Austin's demands and signed a treaty of peace, which, like the Tonkawas and Karankawas, they kept fairly well.

Austin's talk to the Wacos showed his method of dealing with the Indians. It was severe but just, with swift and terrible punishment for violations of their treaties. He expected his settlers to keep their part of the bargain, too, and several times punished colonists who did not treat the Indians fairly.

Austin had to pay the cost of these expeditions against the Indians himself, for the Texas government was not organized well enough to take care of the expense of buying guns and ammunition, food for the men while they were away from home, and gifts of friendship for the Indians.

The expeditions were a great expense to Austin, but they were worth it, for the treaties ended the worst of the Indian troubles in the colony, and in less than two years after the beginning of the colony. Of course for several more years there were Indian attacks and robberies occasionally. As Austin wrote, "The Indians are beginning to fear us, but we cannot for some time yet hope for complete peace with them."

10:

San Felipe de Austin

WHILE Austin was dealing with the Indians, he was busy, too, carrying on the other affairs of his colony. Always there were half a dozen undertakings going on at the same time.

One of these undertakings was surveying the land chosen by the settlers in order to give them clear titles and issue their certificates of ownership. In this land office business Austin was aided by Baron de Bastrop, the old gentleman who had helped Moses Austin get the contract for the colony, and by Samuel M. Williams, a young man from Louisiana who became Austin's secretary. Williams was of special help to Austin because he could speak Spanish and French as well as English and had a good handwriting for writing the deeds for the settlers and the records of the colony. He also became Austin's close friend.

Frequently Austin led the surveying parties himself, and with him he always took his father's tomahawk. These surveying trips had both the fun and the hardships of camping out, and the thrill of danger from wild animals and Indians as well. But there was plenty of plain hard work, too, as the men walked over endless prairie land or cut their way through wilderness, measuring the land, blazing trees, and putting up markers. As they traveled, Austin made notes for a map, which after several years he completed and printed as the first map of Texas.

Another important undertaking for the colony was the establishment of the town which the Mexican government had authorized. By the fall of 1823 Austin had decided on the place for this town, which was to be the capital of his colony, and named it San Felipe de Austin. It was on the Brazos, at a point where a man named McFarland had already started a settlement and established a ferry.

San Felipe de Austin was on the high west bank of the river, almost sixty feet above the water. The town was built around a square or plaza, but the houses were scattered irregularly about the township, not lined up neatly along straight streets. There was a town well, which supplied all the households with water.

Among the earliest businesses were a livery stable where horses could be rented by travelers looking for a place to settle, two wagon yards for keeping wagons in good repair; a grog shop which sold whisky, rum, coffee, and sugar; and a store which sold rice, lard, flour, and cheap cloth.

At the edge of town was another business, "broncho busting." There a pen was filled with wild horses captured by horse hunters or traded from Indians. Young men broke these mustangs and trained them as saddle horses. Then they sold or traded the horses, generally to new settlers who wanted to ride over the countryside and explore the land before selecting their homestead.

In time the town boasted a tavern (which in those days was a hotel), a blacksmith shop, and a printing office. This shop printed the official papers for Austin's colony and did away with the slow work of writing them by hand. Later it published a newspaper, *The Texas Gazette*.

Austin's home in San Felipe was a two-room log cabin built with a runway or dogtrot. Oak pegs were used in it instead of nails, which were scarce in Texas then, and it was caulked with Spanish moss from the trees along the river. One room was Austin's bedroom, the other his office.

Austin might have had a fine two-story house like Colonel Jared E. Groce's nearby plantation home. This was an imposing and beautiful place, with walls of cottonwood logs a foot square, polished as smooth as glass. Across its fifty-five-foot front ran a porch with posts of solid walnut, polished too. There was a sandstone fireplace in each room, and luxurious rugs and beautiful furniture and curtains, brought the long way through the wilderness to the banks of the Brazos.

Some of the colonists thought that Austin, as *empresario*, should have a stately mansion like Colonel Groce's. But Austin decided that his home should be simple, like his neighbors', as were the buckskin clothes he wore.

"It will set an example to the rest of the settlers," he wrote his mother. "We are all poor in this country, and therefore all on an equality, and so long as this continues we shall go on well and harmoniously."

Austin shared his home with his brother, James Brown Austin. Brown, as he was generally called, was ten years younger than Stephen, and Stephen was like a father to him. Brown was a handsome, popular young man, full of high spirits, quick to see the funny side of life, but quick to become bored and depressed also. He called himself Stephen's wild, rattlebrain brother, and his sister Emily described him as a lazy fellow without his father's pride and ambition. But he was a great help to his brother Stephen.

Brown rode through the country on many a necessary errand for Stephen. He kept an eye on affairs in San Felipe while Stephen was away from home on a surveying trip or an expedition against Indians, and he had a way of mingling with the settlers and learning their needs and opinions that resulted in valuable information for Stephen. Sometimes he gave his brother surprisingly good advice from one so much younger, and his light-hearted joking could almost always make Stephen forget his worries about the colony for a little while.

But most of all Brown helped by just being Stephen's family, for the brothers were deeply devoted to each other.

The family had always held an important place in Stephen's life. When he was still in his teens he had taken over the responsibilities of the family, managing his father's business and working hard to pay off its debts.

Then too, the whole Texas venture was undertaken as a family matter, out of loyalty to his father's last wish.

During the long months in Mexico, Stephen had enlarged his idea of the family to include all his colonists. "I feel the same interest for you all which I would for a brother," he wrote them. And again, "I have felt to all the settlers as though they were all my relations, and I look upon them as one great family who are under my care."

But when he returned to Texas he found that he could not

count on his settlers for the warm and satisfying personal relationships that are a part of famly life. For when he became very friendly with one family, others grew jealous and were quick to accuse him of favoritism.

He realized that for the sake of harmony in the colony he must not form close friendships. This knowledge hurt Austin. All his life he had had many friends. Being with his friends was one of the main pleasures of his life, and he felt very lonely now without them.

As soon as he could, he sent for his mother, his sister Emily, and his aunt — all three widows — and Emily's four young children. There'd be no loneliness in a household with four lively youngsters. Besides, he wanted to help Emily with her three sons and little daughter.

In spring, 1824, Austin sent Brown with a caravan of wagons to bring them all to Texas. Full of plans for their happy home in San Felipe, he wrote a long list of instructions for making their overland journey easier and a long list of things to bring with them for their new home.

"Bring all your books and bedding," he began, and gave advice about sending his mother's piano. Then he listed mosquito bars, lead, shot, blacksmith tools, cloth, spices, foods. So many things were needed in Texas that had to come the long way by wagon from Natchitoches or by steamboat from New Orleans.

He asked them to bring supplies for his business with the colony, too: law books; red, white and green flannel for a flag; red, white and green ribbon for a rosette; paper of good quality for deeds to the land; and a large blank book for records.

He made a very special request for seeds and plants to start the garden for the home he planned. He listed the seeds he wanted: cabbage, lettuce, beets, sage, summer savory, and horse radish. Then he asked for roots of orange, fig, grape, and double rose plants, stones of nectarines and peaches, gooseberry, currant, and cypress vines, a dozen young pears and apples, and enough crab apple slips to start a hedge.

In imagination he could see the home they would have together. It would be a simple, substantial log house, roomy and comfortable, set among gardens. And Emily's children would be laughing and playing on the lawn. But the home would have to wait until they came. For the present he was too busy with the colony to start building a house.

He had almost completed settling the first three hundred families his contract called for, and was planning for the second three hundred. Every day new families moved to Texas, and with every family Austin's duties grew heavier.

"In the first place," he said once, explaining his duties, "I have to receive in my household most of those who come to see the country preparatory to moving, entertain them, spend days and weeks going over the land with them; to furnish them translations of the laws and explain them. After all this, when the colonist arrives with his family to settle, the law requires him to present a certificate of character. All these documents are in English or French, and I have the labor of translating them to Spanish.

"After the new colonist is received and has selected his land, the surveyor must survey it; and none of the surveyors understands a word of Spanish, nor does the Land Commissioner understand a word of English. Consequently, I, of necessity, have to supervise everything. The *empresario* has to do the work of a pack mule and carry all the load."

Often Austin thought this load of work and worry almost too heavy to bear. Often when he came home dead tired and found his house cold and untidy, with a stranger on the doorstep waiting to be entertained, he felt that he couldn't go on. Then, "I can stand this a few more weeks," he told himself. "In a few more weeks Mother and Emily will be here, and everything will be better."

And so when he rode across the land or lay too tired to sleep, he dreamed of the home he would have when his family came. Sometimes he saw himself romping with his young nephews, sometimes gardening, sometimes in quiet conversation with his mother. But mostly he imagined them all grouped around his mother's piano, singing. And he counted the days till the wagons would come rolling in with them.

But the wagons came back empty.

A letter from Brown told why. Their mother had died suddenly a few days before they were to start for Texas; their aunt had died a few weeks later, and Emily had decided to marry again and stay in Missouri.

And so Austin put aside his dreams and schooled himself to be patient under discomfort. Bravely, he even tried to joke about his lonely life when he wrote to wish Emily happiness in her second marriage.

"My lot is cast in the wilderness, but I am content," he said; "trouble and fatigue have become so familiar to me that they begin to appear like bosom friends. . . . I am still very poor and live poor — corn coffee, corn bread, milk and butter and a bachelor's household, which is confusion, dirt, and torment — your marriage will force either Brother or me to marry, for I must have somebody to keep house. So you have made a lucky escape, for my house is a thoroughfare for the whole country."

His house was indeed a thoroughfare for the whole country. Even when he was away on a surveying trip or an Indian expedition, travelers stayed in his home. He found a manservant named Simon and an old black woman to cook and clean and help him take care of all these visitors.

Many of these guests were prospective settlers. Some were Mexican officials coming to inspect the colony or bring news from the authorities at San Antonio or Saltillo. Others were colonists with problems and troubles. Still others were Indians on ceremonious visits.

Austin never quite knew whether to be amused or annoyed by these Indian visits, for they were frequent and followed the same pattern. But with his usual tact and understanding, he treated each visit seriously, because he knew it was an important occasion for the Indians and a help in keeping them friendly.

Men, women, and children of the tribe came on these visits. Usually their bodies were painted according to the custom of the

tribe, and they wore ornaments made of beads, shells, and feathers. They always carried a peace pipe, often an elaborate one trimmed with white beads.

Unless the delegation was too large, the visit started with the Indians filing into Austin's office. Austin stood at the door, and each Indian paused for a ceremonious handshake with him, a handshake that jerked his whole arm and left his hand aching. Then as many as could seated themselves on chairs and tables, and the others sat on the floor. When all were seated, Austin passed tobacco, and they smoked in silence until Austin asked them their business. Then they would choose one of the group to speak for them, discussing who it would be in their own language. After they had agreed upon a speaker, he would make a speech, which would then be interpreted for Austin. These speeches told of some complaint or request, generally stressed their desire for peace, and nearly always expressed sorrow that the Great Father had not given the red men the power to read and write.

After the Indian had finished, Austin would make a speech in reply, ending by inviting them to a feast. After the feast the Indians were given presents of tobacco, cloth, rice, beads, and trinkets. Jew's harps and black silk handkerchiefs were favorite gifts.

Indians, American settlers, Mexican officials — all found a welcome in Austin's home. Indeed during the six years he lived at San Felipe not a day passed without visitors.

Often these visitors were troublesome or boring, just a part of his work. But sometimes the guests provided him with good company too.

The more rare visitors to Austin's home were men of equal intelligence and curiosity. To such men Austin would listen eagerly, learning news from San Antonio, from the United States, or from far-off Mexico City. Then, encouraged by the other's interested questions, he would tell of his plans for making Texas great. Such conversations gave him hope again when his goals seemed far from reach. He would talk so enthusiastically and persuasively that his visitors might see in their mind's eye great cities rising in splendor from the prairies, roads teeming with wagons hauling cotton to busy harbors where ships rode at anchor, waiting to carry Texas products to New Orleans or Vera Cruz.

The hour would grow late while Austin and his guests made conversation. The candle would grow short, the remains of the fire would sift to ashes, and finally the chill would force the gathering to retire for the night.

Such evenings made up to Austin for many a dull visitor. When his friends urged him to get rid of the constant stream of guests by giving up his home and renting a room, he refused.

"Keeping bachelor's hall is hard," he agreed. "But I am fully compensated for it by the society of such men as Zavala and Grayson."

11:

A New Government

WHEN Austin first came to Texas, he expected to amass a fortune for himself. But in a few years he had given up that idea. He found it much more interesting and satisfying to plan for the happiness and prosperity of hundreds of settlers — later, of thousands — than merely to make money for himself. Besides, he felt it his duty to work for the colonists because he had brought them to Texas.

But his work for Texas was more than a duty. It was an exciting adventure to him.

Many times he said that as soon as he could, he wanted to withdraw from public life and become a farmer. But perhaps his cousin Henry Austin knew him better than Austin knew himself. "You and I are alike," Henry told him. "We think we would enjoy living quietly on a farm, but we would never be satisfied there. We need some great and important work to keep us happy."

His work for Texas filled this need for Stephen Austin.

Besides the land business and the Indian problem, Austin had to deal with the problem of laws, and as the colony grew, this problem grew with it.

When the colony began, the Mexican government had given Austin complete power to make the laws for the colony and also to enforce these laws. If Austin had been a dictator, he would have liked this plan very much, for it gave him complete power in the government. But he was not a dictator. He did not like so much responsibility and did not approve of it. Like his settlers, he was used to the American system of having one group of people make the laws, another group interpret these laws, and still another enforce them. Furthermore, like his settlers, he believed in trial by jury, a system which the Mexican laws did not recognize.

Austin knew that no matter how careful he was in making laws for the colony and acting as judge when these laws were broken, sooner or later some colonist would suspect him of being deliberately unjust, especially since all legal matters had to be in Spanish, which very few of the settlers understood. Furthermore, there was no book of Spanish laws Austin could use in making his decisions, or show the colonists to prove he was right.

"A person in office should never, at any time, act officially while under the influence of irritation or passion," Austin said. "He ought to execute the law calmly and firmly, but not passionately. And he should do his duty totally regardless of clamor or abuse. My own temper is hasty to a fault and violent when excited, and I therefore laid down the above rule for my own government when I first began the colony."

At first there were few legal problems in the colony. Austin was firm in having every settler present a certificate showing his good character before admitting him to the colony, and as a whole the Texans of his colony had higher standards and were better behaved than the people in an average town.

"When you come here," Austin wrote in 1829, "you will be astonished to see all our houses with no other fastening than a wooden pin or door latch, even stores are left in this state — there is no such thing in the colony as a stable to lock up horses nor pens to guard them in."

Another time he said, "In proportion to our numbers we are as enlightened, as good, and as 'lawbiding' men as can be found in any part of the United States, and greatly more so than ever settled a frontier."

Most of the first questions of law that Austin had to decide were about the ownership of cows or pigs that had strayed. Austin disliked having to decide between neighbors in these disputes, and soon he appointed assistants called alcaldes to help him with the legal problems of the settlement. Then by 1824 he had worked out a system of laws to help him and to guide the alcaldes in their duties.

Most of the offenses were stealing, disturbing the peace, or mistreating the Indians. These offenses were generally punished by fines, public whipping, a sentence to work on some public project such as roads, or banishment from the colony.

But finally two neighbors became so angry at each other that one killed the other. The man said he had fired in self-defense, but the widow claimed her husband had been murdered and demanded that the killer be tried and punished.

This crime showed how much a definite legal system was needed in the colony, for neither Austin nor his alcaldes had power to try murder cases. They could order the accused person to be kept in prison, but they had to send more than five hundred miles to Saltillo to the Mexican court for a decision in the case. This was true not only of murder cases but also of all important legal questions.

Besides objecting to the long delay in punishing crimes, the Texans were annoyed by the Mexican habit of strict observance of rules and forms, which added to the delay. Any legal question sent to the court at Saltillo had to follow exactly a certain form. If there was a mistake in the wording, even in spelling or punctuation, all the papers were sent the long way back to be rewritten. Of course this meant a delay of several months more.

The colonists thought that prompt decision and punishment were more important than correct writing. As a result, they sometimes took matters in their own hands, appointed a jury, and let it decide the case.

One such case happened in Brazoria, a new town on the

coast, which was growing rapidly because the trade from New Orleans came through it. Every house was filled, and merchants' goods often had to be kept on porches or piled in open lots for weeks at a time until a store could be built. All this time the boxes were unguarded, but there were no thefts.

One day, however, two men stole a barrel of whiskey, hid it in a thicket near town, and sneaked there to drink it. One time they got drunk and stabbed a man to death.

If the colonists had followed the regular procedure, it would have been months before these thieves and murderers could be tried. But the citizens of Brazoria were too angry for that delay. They named a jury, which sentenced the two men to be whipped and sent out of Texas.

Austin knew that if the settlers continued to take the law into their own hands like this, it would be dangerous for the colony. Even though the results were good in some cases, soon the men would feel that they could disobey any law that they chose. Therefore he worked hard to get the Mexican government to approve a constitution for Texas. If Texas had a constitution, its government would be based on law, and the danger of mob rule would be ended.

Austin discussed his plans for a constitution with leading colonists, wrote a constitution, and succeeded in persuading the Mexican government to let Texas adopt it. He was very happy when, on February 3 and 4, 1828, in the first election in Texas, the people adopted this constitution and elected their first state officers.

This constitution gave Texas a stronger, more dependable government, especially concerning the towns that were growing so rapidly, and set forth rules for conducting the affairs of these towns. But Mexico still would not permit trial by jury and still demanded that important legal matters be taken the long way to Saltillo. The result was a lasting dissatisfaction among the colonists on these points.

Austin was very glad that the Texans at last had a constitution. It relieved him of many hard duties and responsibilities by setting up departments of the governments to handle them, though he was still held responsible for the government of the colony by the Mexican authorities. The constitution also proved that his colony was firmly established on a sound foundation of law.

One law which Austin succeeded in getting the new legislature to pass was a homestead law. It provided that a man's home and the land, tools, and animals he needed to make a living could not be taken away from him to pay his debts, and that Texas settlers could not be sued for debts made before coming to Texas until twelve years had elapsed. He had protected the settlers in this way while he was judge and worked hard for four years to get this protection made into law.

"This is very important," he wrote the Mexican officials, "for if the Settlers can be sued and their property taken here for debts due in the U. States of North America before they have time to establish themselves and make anything they will be totally ruined. They have some of them spent everything they had to move and settle themselves in this uninhabited Country. They will however be able by cultivating Cotton to pay all their Debts if time is given them, but if their Land and property can be taken for those debts it will ruin them. . . . I think the Legislature would promote the prosperity of the Country and do an act of humanity and justice by giving at least Twelve years for all who remove and settle in this State to pay their old debts."

The legislature passed the law he wanted in 1829. It helped many an honest settler get a start toward prosperity so that it was easy for him to pay his old debts. But Austin himself never used this law. Instead of waiting for the twelve years before paying his debts, he paid what he could on them every year.

This was the first homestead law in Mexico or the United States. Ever since, Texas has had a homestead law, and many other states have used it as a model and adopted homestead laws of their own.

"My ambition is to redeem this fine country . . . and convert it into a home for the unfortunate, a refuge from poverty, an asylum for the sufferers from selfish avarice," he had said. This homestead law was one of the practical ways in which he carried out his ambition.

By 1829, when the colony was seven years old, Austin knew that it would live. Its foundations were sure and firm, and it would continue to grow.

There were about 30,000 Americans in Texas then. Several other *empresarios* had begun colonies, the most important one being Green DeWitt's, farther south than Austin's, along the Guadalupe River. There were almost a dozen towns, including ports at Velasco and Galveston.

Trade was flourishing, both by land and by sea. The ports were busy with incoming settlers and outgoing products. Roads had been built so that cotton and supplies could be hauled from one part of the colony to gins or ships, and there was a good carriage road from Alexandria, Louisiana, to San Felipe.

Most of the settlers farmed, and crops were good. One farmer reported that on ninety-three acres cultivated by seven hands he raised eighty bales of cotton, five hundred bushels of sweet potatoes, and two thousand bushels of corn. Another wrote that usually they made two cotton crops a year, that the average height of the cotton on river bottom lands was nine to twelve feet and the yield per acre over two thousand five hundred pounds.

Besides cotton, corn, and sweet potatoes, other important crops were sugar cane, tobacco, indigo, small grains, and vegetables.

Stock raising was becoming another important industry. Austin himself started the first stock farm in his colony. In 1826 he had sent Brown across the Rio Grande to buy some fine horses for the stock farm he planned. After a long, tiresome journey and delays caused by illness, Brown reached Rancho de la Luz, the home of their friend Don Luciano. He was greeted hospitably but was told there was one big obstacle to selling Stephen the horses. A year's bad drought had scattered Don Luciano's herds so that it was almost impossible to round them up. Even if enough horses could be found, the drought would make it impossible to drive them back to San Felipe. Even the water pool at the Rancho was drying up, and animals were dying for lack of water. Don Luciano deplored the situation and invited Brown to be his guest until he had rested for the return journey.

Brown was glad to accept the don's hospitality and enjoyed his visit. Within three days the weather changed suddenly, and in three hours there came the most tremendous torrent of rain

Brown had ever seen. The water rushed from the mountains in such floods that everything was swept before it. In a few hours rivers and lakes were filled with a water supply for a year to come. There was great rejoicing at the rancho that night, and as soon as the weather cleared again they rounded up three hundred head of stock for Austin. With the help of vaqueros, Brown drove these horses back to San Felipe for the first stock farm of the colony.

Now many settlers were raising horses, cattle, and hogs. "It is as easy to raise cattle in Texas," they said, "as to raise chickens."

Industries had started in Texas, too. There were cotton gins, grist mills, and steam sawmills.

Other products were lumber, leather goods, and hides and furs. In 1828, eight thousand dollars' worth of peltry was shipped through Nacogdoches. The furs included beaver, otter, buffalo, badger, bear, deer, and "small leopards." Generally traders got these furs from Indians, but some settlers hunted for a living.

Many of the products were sold or traded among the settlers themselves. But others, especially cotton, were usually loaded on boats and sent to the United States or Mexico. Texas cotton worth ten dollars in New Orleans brought thirty dollars in San Luis Potosi, Mexico.

Texas had a newspaper by 1829, too — *The Texas Gazette,* printed in San Felipe by Godwin Brown Cotton. The first book published in Texas was Austin's translation of the Spanish colonization laws.

One thing Austin felt Texas lacked was a public school system. "A nation can only be free, happy, and great," he wrote, "in proportion to the virtue and intelligence of the people; the dissemination of useful knowledge and of the arts and sciences is therefore of primary importance to national liberty and prosperity."

Austin tried to interest the people in establishing an academy for a hundred pupils at San Felipe. It would be a brick building — Austin himself drew the plans — and Thomas J. Pilgrim, a highly educated man, would be the teacher. But the parents preferred to keep their children at home instead of sending them to school in San Felipe, and so the plan was abandoned.

A few years later Austin prepared a bill for the legislature, providing for an Institute of Modern Languages to be established at San Felipe. This school would teach the Spanish, English, and French languages and also "arithmetic, geography, mathematics, history, rhetoric, constitutional law, philosophy, astronomy, and chemistry." But this law was never passed. The people of the colony were not ready to start public education.

Many of the children, however, attended private schools in the towns. Sometimes in large families living in the country a teacher would be employed to teach the children at home. But many children did not go to school at all.

12:

Colonel Austin

AFFAIRS in the colony were going so well that Austin felt that at last he could give attention to his own affairs. He thought that he could soon finish his business with the colony and devote all his time to his farm — the one he had planned so long. Perhaps it was time to heed his sister's advice to marry. Perhaps, as she suggested, he would go back to Missouri and look up some of the girls he used to know.

"Your old favorite Miss Courtney Baylor is now a widow," Emily wrote him. And again, "Your old flame Miss Isabella Hurd has turned Methodist and is going to heaven as fast as possible."

Austin was still a young man, but the seven years of over-work and worry had been hard on him. Brown wrote Emily, "He begins to look quite old and the wrinkles are becoming plainer daily."

Brown was happily married by this time. He and his wife Eliza had a handsome baby boy, eight months old, named in honor of his Uncle Stephen. Austin loved this child dearly and was very proud to have a namesake. As often as he could, he visited Brown's little family.

He had helped his brother start a new merchandising business. They had bought a boat, the *Eclipse,* to trade between Texas and New Orleans, and Brown was living on a farm near Brazoria.

In August, 1829, Brown sailed on the *Eclipse* to New Orleans on a business trip. When he had been there only a few days, he became ill of yellow fever and died.

At the same time Stephen fell ill, very ill, in Texas.

When they told him of his brother's death, he was so sick that they were not sure that he understood. For days he lay unconscious, but somehow he knew of his brother's death and fought grief as well as disease. His friends were afraid he would die, too, but slowly he recovered.

He returned to a world of weariness and sorrow. His work was waiting for him, piled up on his desk. There was a new decree from Mexico that he was sure would mean trouble for the colony, a decree abolishing slavery, but every effort exhausted him, every effort seemed so useless now that Brown was gone and he was alone.

His only comfort was his namesake, Brown's little son.

When he held the baby, his grief was eased a little. He would be a father to little Stephen, he decided. As soon as the child was a little older, he would adopt him and raise him as his own son. Everything he had hoped to do for his brother, he would do now for his brother's son. Eliza, Brown's young widow, understood Austin's sorrow and loneliness, and tried to coax him back to cheerfulness. But Austin only plunged back into his work, trying to forget his loss in planning for his colonists once more.

He thought often of his sister Emily and wished that she and her family could be with him. The idea grew on him so strongly that he wrote urging her to move to Texas.

Always before he had told relatives who had asked about coming to Texas that they must see Texas and judge for themselves. Indeed, that is what he urged all prospective settlers, for he did not want anyone to move to Texas and then be disappointed and unhappy. But now he put aside this policy and asked Emily and her husband, James F. Perry, to move to Texas.

His letter was written on New Year's Eve, 1829. It was like a cry of despair rising from his grief and need of love. "I am quite alone here," he said. "I have set my heart on your removal and I shall be dreadfully disappointed if you do not prepare to move, for I must have you here. You must come, indeed you *must.*"

This letter to Emily was followed closely by one from Eliza. "If Stephen was sure you would move in the spring he would fatten up and be a different man," she wrote. "He is now nothing but a mere shadow, and if he does not quit his desk, ride about, take more exercise, his life will be but short. Next week he is going out with the Surveyors and will spend a month or more in the woods. He thinks in that time he will regain his health. . . .

"My sister, my constant prayer will be for you to move to this country and cheer Stephen up. I am myself well enough but if you was here to tease and plague him we could make him throw off that gloomy, melancholy look and show a smiling countenance."

Emily faced a hard choice. Should she take her children from the security of Missouri to the uncertainty of Texas? Ask her husband to give up a safe small business there to risk a better one in Stephen's colony?

Reluctantly she made her choice. She would go to her brother in his need.

In April her husband went to Texas to make final plans. When he reached San Felipe he learned that Austin was out with a surveying party and hired guides to lead him to Austin. They found him surveying the land recently granted to the Perrys at Austin's request, a 48,000 acre tract along the coast.

Perry seemed enthusiastic about Texas. Austin pointed out the opportunities for making a fortune in Texas and told Perry, too, how much he needed help with his own business affairs, help that Perry could give him.

"I need you here to manage my money affairs," he told Perry. "I must spend so much time on the affairs of the colony that I have neglected my own affairs entirely. Unless I have someone to manage them for me, I shall be as poor as a church mouse as long as I live."

It was agreed that Perry should help Austin and also run a merchandise business, and that when they had built a home, Austin would live with them. Perry was to go back to Missouri, sell his property there, and bring his family to Texas as soon as possible.

Once more Austin began to plan happily for the reunion of his family. They would build a big house with a wing for him, and Eliza and little Stephen should live with them too.

He wrote his sister about the site of the land he had chosen for her. "It is on the bay and is I think a very handsome and healthy one. The boys can have their fill of fishing, and in the winter wild fowl are numerous. . . . I will give the boys ponies and a little boat, and something pretty to the girls. . . . We must provide a teacher to live in the family and educate them well. By the time they will be coming on to the stage, Texas will present a fine field for men of education and talents. Mr. P. will get Spanish books. They all ought to learn that language."

Once more he wrote a long list of instructions of things to bring. He urged Perry to bring merchandise for his store and goods for the Indians and for a hundred soldiers recently stationed in the colony by Mexico. He asked also for materials for a new uniform for himself. "Uniform that of Colonel of infantry in the Mexican Army, with gold epaulets and gold or yellow mounted sword. . . . I must have a sword, a sash and belt, yellow mounted. I also want a military surtout with a standing collar, handsomely though plainly trimmed with black silk cord and pantaloons trimmed in the same manner — all of navy blue cloth. Also a scarlet westcott with gold round cord on the edges, a pair of boots and yellow spurs. As I am the highest militia officer in Texas it is expected I provide myself with these things."

Once again he asked for seeds and cuttings of plants, and for books. He listed law books, an atlas, and various literature "to try to improve my mind which needs it much, for during the years I have spent in Texas but few books have come within my reach."

And once again he was disappointed.

Late in the summer his sister wrote that Perry had thought Austin cold and unfriendly when they met in Texas and that they had almost changed their minds about coming to Texas.

It was like a slap in the face to Austin. Once more he realized that his dreams for happiness with his family were only dreams, that he must face life alone.

"I was surprised that you thought me silent and reserved," he wrote sadly to Perry. "It was what I never dreamed of. . . . You must not expect to find me the cheerful companion I once was. . . . Never again think that I am silent or cool towards you, for I assure you that there is nothing of that in my heart, nothing."

But he did not again urge them to come to him. Instead he told them that he had just been elected to represent Texas in the state legislature which met five hundred miles away in Saltillo. "I had no idea and no wish for such a thing," he said. "I cordially detest politics in any country." But having been elected, he felt it his duty to go to the legislature. Since this meant that he would have to be away from home for several months, he suggested that the Perrys do nothing about Texas until his return from Saltillo.

13:

Happy Summer

A YEAR had passed since his brother's death
and Stephen's own illness, and during that time Texas had been
progressing almost too well to suit Mexico. Mexican officials
saw how strong and prosperous the colony was becoming and
were afraid they would lose it.

Mexico had hoped that Mexican settlers would move into
Texas in equal numbers with the Americans, but only a handful
did so. Now there were so many Americans in Texas that Mexico
feared they would try to take Texas for the United States. The
fact that the United States had asked to buy Texas and had offered to pay five million dollars for it only made this fear stronger.

The Mexican government decided that to keep Texas they
must stop new settlers from coming to Texas and discourage

those already there. Therefore President Guerrero issued an Emancipation Decree freeing the slaves in Texas. Mexico thought that few Americans would move to Texas without slaves and that the important cotton farmers could not continue to prosper without slave labor.

Almost the first thing Austin heard when he began to recover from his illness was news of this decree, for the colonists were upset and angry about it. He thought it was a good decree and would in the long run be the best thing for the colonists, for he hated slavery, "that curse of curses," as he called it. As soon as he was able to be up and around, he began talking to the settlers and trying to make them see that freeing the slaves would be a good thing for the colony.

But he could not persuade them. "Who will work our fields?" settlers asked. "Who will pick our cotton?"

"Without slave labor," they argued, "we shall be ruined. Mexico wanted us to come here, gave us prize land for settling here. Now that we are making Texas valuable, Mexico is trying to take it away from us by taking away our slaves. You must prevent that."

In this case, as in many others, Austin thought that he knew what was good for the colonists better than they did themselves. But he was not a dictator. He worked hard to make them understand that his way was best, but if he failed to convince them, he accepted their decision and tried to carry out the will of the majority.

That is what he did now about the Emancipation Decree.

After months of dealing with the Mexican authorities, he succeeded in getting a change in the decree. The Texans could keep the slaves they had, but they could bring in no more slaves, and when the children of the slaves reached the age of fourteen, they would become free.

Official news that Texas had been exempted from the Emancipation Decree came on December 24, 1829. But Austin knew that Mexico was still looking for a way to stop immigration to Texas.

One morning in May, 1830, Sam Williams, Austin's secretary, walked into the office to find Austin sagging in his chair, his face drawn and gray.

"Colonel Austin," Williams exclaimed in alarm, "are you ill?"

"Not ill," Austin replied without looking up.

"Why, then, what is the matter?"

Austin lifted a paper from the desk. "This," he said. "I have just received the deathstroke for my colony."

"What do you mean, Colonel?"

"This law passed by the Mexican Congress. The Law of April 6, 1830, they call it. It has done what the Emancipation Decree could not. It halts all American immigration to Texas."

"That is a setback, surely," Williams agreed soothingly, "but not necessarily a deathblow. You will be able to think of some way around it. You always have, when Mexico passed unfavorable laws."

"Only if they were unconstitutional. This one is constitutional. It is cleverly thought out. At one stroke it destroys the colony."

"There are almost thirty thousand people in Texas now. Surely they can still work and prosper."

"For a short time only. Why have men bought land here? In the belief that an ever-growing population will make it valuable. Why have merchants built stores here? In the hope of having more and more people as customers. Why have farmers and doctors and carpenters and blacksmiths and lawyers come here? All in the belief that a growing population will need their services. Immigration is the lifeblood of Texas. When it is cut off, Texas will dwindle and die."

"But why would Mexico do that?"

"You know, Williams. Because it is afraid it will lose Texas. Rather than that, it will kill Texas. But it would not have to lose Texas. Mexico has not within its whole dominions a man who would defend its independence, all its constitutional rights, sooner than I would, or be more ready and willing to discharge his duties as a Mexican citizen. I have been loyal, but I can keep the colony loyal only if Mexico gives us the laws we need and allows us to prosper. But what use is it to talk about it? The colony is done for."

"Is there nothing you can do about this law?"

"Nothing. Read for yourself."

Williams took the paper and began to read aloud, translating as he read. Austin slumped in his chair, staring into space.

"Article 10 and Article 11," Williams said, "what do they

mean? The colonies already established, or the colonies already completed? How would you translate it?"

Suddenly Austin sat erect. "That's it!" he exclaimed. "That's it! Let me read it again."

"Here, but I don't see —"

"This phrase could mean 'an established colony.' My colony is certainly established. And that means that my colony is not subject to the law prohibiting immigration, that the law applies only to colonies that are not firmly settled."

Austin rose, tense with excitement and relief, and began to pace the floor.

"But do you think the Mexicans meant to exempt your colony?"

"I don't know. But I'm going to convince them that they did. This phrase is a loophole. It will enable me to keep the door to Texas open for some time longer, perhaps until there is a new order of things in Mexico."

Immediately he sat down and began the first of many letters to influential Mexicans. In each he took for granted that his interpretation of the law was the correct one and stressed the loyalty of the colonists.

The colonists were, of course, greatly upset when they heard of the Law of April 6, 1830, and they besieged Austin with demands that he safeguard their interests. They elected him to represent them at the legislature in Saltillo. This was the election about which he had written his sister.

After weeks of careful work, soothing the Mexican fears

and calming the settlers' anger, Austin succeeded in persuading the Mexican leaders that his colony and Green DeWitt's, the only ones which had largely completed their contracts, were exempt from the law and could continue to bring in settlers.

In the next few months colonists poured into Austin's and DeWitt's colonies, two and three hundred coming each month. But the other colonies, as Austin had feared, dwindled and died; and their *empresarios* blamed Austin because he could not save them.

Austin returned from the legislature at Saltillo late in the spring of 1831. When he reached San Felipe he learned with pleasure that at last some of his relatives would be near him.

One was his cousin Henry Austin, who had been a cabin boy at sea when Stephen was at school in Connecticut. Henry had really come to Texas two years before, with hopes of making a fortune with his steamship on the Rio Grande. But the Mexicans who lived near the river were afraid of the steamship. They thought it was a strange, powerful animal that at any moment might attack them. They would not ride on it or send their goods by it.

And so the venture failed, but not Henry's faith in Texas. He had now moved to Austin's colony with other plans for making a fortune for his family.

The Henry Austin home was unusual in Texas, for in their simple house with its puncheon floors they placed fine furniture and beautiful china from their New Haven home. The family was unusual, too, for all the children were beautiful and charming, full of eager questions and laughter. Their love for each other, their interest in books and music and the fine courtesies of life made their home a happy place.

Henry Austin's sister, Mary Austin Holley, came to visit them that summer. She and Stephen remembered their Sunday visit when he was a puny schoolboy in Connecticut and immediately struck up a friendship again. Mary Holley, a widow now, was even lovelier than when she was a girl.

She was enthusiastic over Texas and wanted to buy land there, enough to make her wealthy some day. She was also collecting material for a book about Texas, and in her search for information Stephen was her willing guide. He arranged for her to travel through the country, and she was as happy and eager about her new experiences as if each trip were a picnic.

As she grew acquainted with Texas, she realized the greatness of Austin's work there more than his family or his colonists did. Encouraged by her friendly enthusiasm, Austin told her more about his dreams and plans for Texas than he had ever told anyone else.

"I found the country so much more valuable than I expected," he confided to her, "that the idea of contributing to fill it with a civilized and industrious population filled my soul with enthusiasm. . . . For the first time *ambition* kindled its fires in my breast, but I think I can with truth say that the flame was a mild and gentle one, consisting more of the wish to build up the fortunes and happiness of others and to realize my dreams of good will to my fellow men than of the overbearing spirit of

military fame or domineering power."

He told her of his plans for himself, too, of his hope to retire from public service to the colony and settle down to a quiet happy life on a farm near his sister, who had moved to Texas after all.

"I need a social circle," he wrote Mrs. Holley, "a few friends of congenial tastes the want of which left a void. That void is being filled. My sister's family, and Henry's, and Archibald's, and you, my friend, you!"

They planned for comfortable, simple homes with lovely gardens and music and books and the good conversation of friends. "We will be happy," he said. "I am now convinced that I shall enjoy some of the fruits of my planting. . . . On our ponies we will scamper over the flowery prairies to the sea, with friendship and happiness in our hearts."

Whenever he could, that summer, Austin talked with Mary Holley, rode with her on her explorations, and danced with her at the balls which were becoming more frequent in Texas. When they were apart, they wrote to each other. Women in the colony began to think that at last Austin would marry.

Emily thought so, too, and was pleased. She and her family had arrived in Texas shortly after Austin's return from Saltillo, and he was busy and happy helping to get them settled and becoming acquainted all over again with his sister and her husband and his two nieces and five nephews.

Some of the children he was seeing for the first time. The oldest was sixteen, and the youngest was born after they reached Texas. Austin immediately took Moses Austin Bryan, his oldest nephew, under his wing to train him as his private secretary.

Austin's happiness in their arrival was dimmed a little because Emily seemed dissatisfied with Texas. She complained about the crudeness and discomforts of life in San Felipe and worried about the mosquitoes and fevers that attacked so many settlers each summer.

Austin thought she should overlook these things and keep her mind on the great future they would soon be enjoying.

"You let trifles too much influence you," he told her. "A puncheon hut or an Indian camp is nothing, a mere trifle, when it is to be only a stepping place to get into a comfortable home and farm for life. . . . Your removal to Texas will make your children all independent, which they would never have been in Missouri."

If Austin thought her fretful, she undoubtedly thought him bossy. For he had been planning and deciding for a whole colony so long that he had gotten into the habit of telling those nearest him what to do.

He even tried to settle the futures of the boys. He wanted little Stephen and Emily's son Guy "to study law so as to take care of the future interests of the family. . . . They must learn Spanish and French, and send all the children to dancing school. Joel ought to be brought up for a planter and Austin for a merchant. Your Stephen and Henry are too young yet to say what they are best calculated for."

Austin had counted greatly on the help his brother-in-law would be to him. "Unless I can get some rest," he had written the summer before, "I shall not live much longer, for I am nearly worn down — for nine years since I came to Texas my mind has had no rest, nothing to relieve it from continued cares and anxieties."

Another time he had told Perry, "I am laboring more for yours and Emily's children than for myself. What do I want with property or fortune? But little will do me, and every year less."

But at first Perry and his family were more of an added burden than a help, for they depended on Austin to settle them in their new home and start them in a successful business. They could not decide where they wanted to live. Finally, against Austin's advice, they started a store at Chocolate Bayou.

But that came later. This first summer they were all happy and excited, getting to know one another and making fine plans for the future. To Mary Austin Holley and the Perry children, life in Texas was a thrilling adventure.

It was the pleasantest summer Austin had ever spent in Texas, but a very busy one. For besides his new social activities he had to attend to all his regular business of the colony, and there was more than usual. Now settlers were pouring into his colony and Green DeWitt's, afraid that if they waited, the Mexican government might shut off colonization entirely.

Two and three hundred settlers a month came to Austin's colony, and Austin had the main work of helping them find land and giving them titles to it.

But another big task for him that year was trying to keep peace between the colonists and the government, for men were growing more and more upset over the Law of April 6, 1830. Austin was afraid their dissatisfaction would turn to violence, and he did everything he could to convince the settlers that they must be patient and work out their problems by peaceful means.

As usual, he overworked. In the fall he became ill and almost died, for the second time in three years. It took him many weeks to get his strength back, but this time he had nieces and nephews to wait on him and amuse him and Emily to serve him delicious nourishing broths and custards.

While he was getting strong, he spent ten never-to-be-forgotten days in the home of his cousin Henry, where Mary Austin Holley was also a guest. The gaiety of this affectionate family, the music and laughter and good talk, were what Austin had been needing for years. "A more lovely or beautiful family I have never seen," he wrote home, "so blooming and cheerful."

He confided too that he thought Mary Austin Holley "a divine woman, the most agreeable company I have met with for many years."

The visit was a delightful experience, and they all hoped it could be repeated often, but as soon as he was able Austin had to leave again to attend the legislature in Saltillo. Before he left he paid a visit to Emily.

"I reached home night before last," he wrote in telling Mary Holley of this visit, "after riding forty-seven miles that day and found sister Emily at a ball, dancing away in fine spirits. She enjoyed the party, and I joined her, caught the excitement, remembered your injunction 'laugh away care' and soon forgot my forty-seven mile ride."

Austin was always pleased when Emily was happy, and her happiness added to his pleasure in the dance. He enjoyed dancing and was always popular at these events. He was a graceful dancer, always elegantly dressed, always courtly in manner, and almost always he was the most powerful and important man present. All the young ladies felt very much honored if he invited them to dance and wrote about a dance with Austin as an outstanding incident of the evening. One young dance partner — she was only twelve years old — described Austin as a dry little bachelor, but even when she was an old lady she remembered her dance with him as one of her triumphs of the affair.

14:

An Unpopular Law

WHEN Austin returned from the legislature at Saltillo in July, 1832, everything was different. Mary Holley had gone back to her home. Emily was discontented with her life in the colony and blamed Austin for persuading them to come. And the colonists had come to actual fighting with the Mexican government.

As Austin had feared, the Perry business at Chocolate Bayou had not proved successful. Finally Austin took matters in his own hands and decided that they should make their home at Peach Point. But Emily still complained about the hardships of their life and the lack of recognition for Stephen's work. Her unhappiness grieved Austin. He tried to cheer her up, but at the same time he felt that he must work all the harder to make conditions in Texas more to her liking.

"It distracts me to see you unhappy," he told her. "Everything has turned out differently from what I expected when I first wrote Perry to move, but if you were satisfied I should not be at all discouraged at the present state of things. This country must prosper in the end; it cannot be otherwise. This year has been bad — unusually wet, and filled with trouble, but next year will be much better. This world is all trouble, or not so bad, just as we choose to make it — content is everything."

It was hard for Austin himself not to feel that the world was all trouble the next few months. For while he was gone, the colonists had become more and more upset and angry about the Law of April 6, 1830, and some were saying, "If Mexico will not give us our rights, we will take them by force."

Besides the provision of the law stopping new settlers from coming from the United States, the settlers objected to other parts of the law. One was the stationing of Mexican soldiers in Texas to collect taxes and enforce the laws, these soldiers to be supported at the expense of the Texans. Another was a series of taxes and duties planned to force the Texans to trade with Mexico rather than the United States.

For another thing, the colonists were demanding to be separated from Coahuila, the Mexican state of which they had been a part since 1824. Coahuila was just across the Rio Grande River, but it was very different from Texas in the kind of people who lived there, the kind of country and climate, and the products and industries; and the capital, Saltillo, was five hundred miles from the main Texas settlements.

The Mexican government made laws for Texas and Coahuila together, and Texans thought it unfair that they should have to obey laws which benefited Coahuila but hurt Texas. They wanted to be a separate state with their own laws, judges who understood English, and the right of trial by jury.

The Mexican government had promised Texas statehood as soon as it was strong enough. Now that their population had passed thirty thousand, Texans thought that Mexico should keep this promise.

The Law of April 6, 1830, was unpopular enough. But to make matters worse, Mexico appointed several disagreeable and overbearing men to enforce this law. These men made regulations which the settlers considered unnecessary, unreasonable, and insulting. One of these rules, for instance, required that all ship captains must pay the duty on their ships at Anahuac, a customs office so far from the place where they usually landed that it meant a two-hundred-mile ride overland before they could set sail again.

This and many other dictatorial decrees angered the colonists so much that several small groups had fought the Mexican officials, and in the shooting, men had been killed.

Austin still believed that the best way to solve the problem was by peaceful, lawful means. He worked hard, on the one hand trying to persuade the settlers to keep calm and use only legal methods to get what they wanted, and on the other hand to convince the Mexican government that Texas was a loyal colony asking only for what it needed and deserved. He traveled from one part of Texas to another talking with influential people, and he wrote hundreds of letters to those he could not see personally in Texas and Mexico.

He tried especially to get the Mexican Texans at San Antonio to take the lead in demanding the changes that all Texas wanted, for he knew that their requests and demands would be heeded in Mexico much sooner than the American Texans'.

But some of the Texans, too angry and impatient to work quietly, interfered with this plan. They called a convention in 1832 and another in 1833 to discuss their problem. Austin was afraid that Mexico would consider these conventions treason and did what he could to prevent hotheaded warlike action. As he expected, the Mexicans from San Antonio refused to attend the convention, knowing that the Mexican government would consider it an insult, if not downright treason.

Austin made himself personally unpopular because he tried to influence Texans to let the San Antonio Mexicans take the lead in dealing with Mexico. He said, "I considered that very great respect and deference was justly due to them as native Mexicans, as the capital of Texas, and as the oldest and most populous town in the country, and I knew the importance of getting them to take the lead in all the politics of Texas. Besides this, I was personally attached to those people as a sincere friend."

But the convention would not listen to him on this subject, for as Austin wrote later, "At that time it was death to any man's popularity to speak in favor of the Mexicans."

The second convention, meeting in April, 1833, went so far as to adopt a constitution for Texas as a separate state and elected three men to take this constitution to the government at Mexico City for approval and to get the law of April 6, 1830, repealed.

Two of the men decided that they could not leave their families and businesses for as long a time as the trip would take, and the third man, Austin, had to go alone.

He did not want to go, either. "This trip to Mexico interferes very much with me," he wrote his sister. "In two months more I could have closed all my business and gone to work improving a farm, and I intended to do so."

But as always, Austin placed his duty to the colonists above his own welfare and prepared to go alone on the long journey. He knew he would be gone at least four months, but he made plans to take care of all his business as if he were to be gone much longer, almost as if he thought he might never return. He gave his favorite little gray horse to his sister, a saddle and bridle to his brother-in-law, and some of his clothes to his nephews. He wrote instructions for the education of little Stephen and said he wanted his father's tomahawk saved for the little boy. "I have the tomahawk that Father had with him on his first trip to Texas in my trunk," he wrote. "I wish it preserved and its history not forgotten. It blazed the way for North Americans to Texas. . . . I have also carried it on most of my exploring trips in early times. The recollections connected with it are very interesting to me."

Much more now than when he had made the trip to Mexico ten years before, he realized the dangers that lay ahead of him. But after only a week of hurried preparations he set out on the mission. "I am on the wing for twelve hundred miles," he wrote Mary Holley just before he left, "on a mule's back (not a pegasus) over plains and mountains, to the City of Montezuma, farther from all hopes of farm and home than I ever was."

He went first to San Antonio and then to Goliad, trying to get the Mexican citizens there to sign petitions for him to take to Mexico. He knew such papers would have great weight with the Mexican authorities. But though the Mexicans in both towns were in favor of the demands of the convention, they would not sign petitions. And so the first step of his journey was disappointing.

More unpleasantness awaited him on the road ahead. He had word that Indians had recently killed two men not far from San Antonio, and he had to keep alert for danger along the road. Rain made traveling uncomfortable, and he had to cope with muddy roads and swollen creeks and rivers.

When he reached Matamoras, Austin decided it would be pleasanter to go to Vera Cruz by boat than to go the long land route. But the voyage turned out to be very disagreeable. There were storms on the Gulf of Mexico and the little schooner was blown off her course. Instead of one week, it took four to reach Vera Cruz. Because of the unexpected delay, food and water had to be rationed. Austin was miserably seasick the whole time.

From Vera Cruz to Mexico City there were more troubles. At one place the road was blocked by rebel soldiers. At another he was delayed because an official at Vera Cruz had forgotten to sign his passport and it seemed for a time that he would have to go all the way back for the signature. But finally on July 18, 1833, he reached Mexico City, almost three months from the day he had left San Felipe.

Austin found life in Mexico City at a standstill because of a terrible epidemic of cholera. Congress had adjourned, and there was little he could do but wait for the epidemic to pass over and Congress to meet again.

When he arrived in the city, Austin himself was still weak from a mild attack of the dreaded disease. As soon as he felt the symptoms he took a remedy that was recommended to him and believed that it saved his life.

The cholera raged for weeks. About forty-three thousand people had it, and more than eighteen hundred died. "I never witnessed such a horrible scene of distress and death," Austin wrote.

All during this time of horror Austin was worried about conditions in Texas, for in the four months since he had left home he had received only one letter. Why didn't his sister or Perry write? Why didn't Williams report on the state of the colony? Were the politicians keeping quiet and trusting him to solve Texas problems, or were they inflaming the settlers to new acts of violence? And what of his family? Had cholera struck in Texas too? Was the colony wiped out?

Austin watched every mail, but no letter came for him.

By October the epidemic in Mexico City had ended and Congress was in session again. Austin tried to forget his worries in working for the repeal of the Law of April 6, 1830, and for Texas statehood. The results were discouraging.

He felt that the time for cautious, complimentary speech was over. He said openly, "Either the local government of Texas should be reorganized or Mexico should sell Texas to the United States while she can at least make a profit from Texas. If Mexico does neither, she is in danger of losing Texas."

Many prominent men agreed with him, but Congress hesitated to act, partly because President Santa Anna was away from the city, leading the army to crush a rebellion. Valentin Gomez Farias was acting president but could not or did not act on the matter.

And so the days dragged on, full of worry about friends and relatives in Texas and discouragement and delays in the business for Texas, until October 2. That day at last two letters came for Austin. Both held terrible news. One told of cholera sweeping Texas, bringing death to some of his best friends, to Henry Austin's wife and his sister Emily's little daughter. The other had news of more political trouble in Texas.

Half sick with grief and worry, Austin had to keep an appointment with Vice-President Farias. For once he forgot the polite formalities of Mexican interviews and spoke bluntly. Farias felt insulted, and the meeting ended angrily.

Austin went to his room and, sad and disheartened, answered his letters. To his brother-in-law he wrote, "I am so much afflicted by accounts of the deaths by cholera in Texas that I can scarcely write anything. . . . I am too wretched to write much on this subject or any other."

And to the authorities at San Antonio he wrote, "Nothing has been done, and I regret to say that in my opinion nothing will be done. . . . In this belief I hope that you will not lose a moment in urging all the *ayuntamientos* of Texas to unite in organizing a local government independent of Coahuila, even though the general government refuses its consent."

In a few days, when Austin had recovered from the shock of the bad news from Texas, he apologized to Vice-President Farias, and the two were on friendly terms again. But the damage had been done.

Soon Santa Anna returned, victorious, and when Austin had an interview with him, he seemed to be in favor of granting all the colonists' requests. In fact, with Santa Anna's support, Congress agreed to all except the request for statehood for Texas and seemed to favor that also. But Austin could tell that they were not ready to grant statehood now.

Happy that he had at least secured the repeal of the hated Law of April 6, 1830, Austin decided that he had accomplished everything possible for the present and on December 10 set out for home, eager to comfort his relatives in their sorrow, to wind up his work for the colony, and to settle at last on his own farm.

15:

Austin in Prison

T HE trip promised to be his most pleasant one on the road between Mexico City and San Felipe. This time he traveled in a coach accompanied by three Spanish dons and their servants. He took time to visit the churches and convents in the towns where they stopped, and admired their beauty and splendor. He enjoyed the delicious sweetmeats sold by the nuns and collected seeds from the convent gardens to plant on his farm.

He kept a journal of this trip, with the following entry for December 17, 1833:

"At dusk Don Miguel suddenly entered the room and told us that the Robbers were scheming with the coachmen to rob us on the following day. All the company became alarmed, and Don Luis determined to go to the political chief and ask him

for an escort. I was opposed to it. I did not believe the story about the robbers. They replied that I was not acquainted with the country or the people, that it was full of robbers." The political chief gave them an escort "and on the following day we set out in great state, coach and six soldiers on horseback as an escort, with their lances and red flags." The robbers did not attack, and the time passed pleasantly.

On January 3 they reached Saltillo, and Austin went to the governor's office to talk over Texas affairs. When he walked in he was arrested by General Lemus on the order of Vice-President Farias.

"There must be some mistake," Austin said in surprise.

"No, Colonel Austin," General Lemus replied. "There is no mistake."

"But why? What have I done?"

"You perhaps know better than I, Colonel Austin."

"But I do not know. I have done nothing."

"You wrote a letter to the San Antonio officials on October 2."

"Yes. What about it?"

"That letter is the cause of your arrest. It was sent to Vice-President Farias, and he considers it very bad. He thinks it was written to urge the colonists to revolt against Mexico."

"Oh, no," Austin denied, shocked by the accusation. "Not to start a revolt. To prevent one."

"It is difficult to see, Colonel Austin, how the letter asking the San Antonians to take the lead in forming a state government could be called an attempt to stop a revolt."

"But don't you see, General Lemus, that if the Mexicans take the lead they will bring about the reform within the Mexican government. But if the Americans take the lead, their first step will be to break away from the Mexican government."

"I see your point," General Lemus replied slowly but in a more friendly tone. "It may be that you are right. At any rate, it is my painful duty to arrest you and take you back to Mexico City."

"But with what crime am I charged?"

"I do not know, Colonel Austin. When you reach Mexico City, you will doubtless be informed. In the meantime let us not discuss it. I shall treat you as my guest. You shall return to the capital in the carriage with my family."

They had not gone far on their return journey when a bitterly cold north wind blew up and filled the sky with gray clouds. But Austin felt that the weather was no colder or gloomier than his future.

After the first shock of the arrest, his thoughts had been of Texas. What would his arrest mean to Texas? Almost certainly it would be the spark that would set fire to the discontent of the colonists, and war would soon be raging.

Were all his years of quiet work for the peaceful growth of Texas to be wasted now in one instant? Was his colony to be destroyed by war and all his labor and sacrifice lost? The thought was too bitter. He must prevent such a war, whatever the result for him personally.

As they rode, Austin was busy thinking through this problem. But all the while he tried to keep up a polite friendly conversation with General Lemus and his family, who acted as if he were their honored guest instead of their prisoner. When they reached Monterey, where General Lemus had business, Austin asked for permission to write to his family and friends.

He wrote till his hand ached that day, for he did not know when he would be allowed to write again. He completed and mailed fifteen long, important letters. And all emphasized that

Texans must not let his arrest lead them to hasty action.

"Give yourself no kind of uneasiness about this matter," he wrote to his sister and brother-in-law. "It can do me no harm other than the delay and expense. It is very likely that I may be hammered and pummeled about for a year before I get home again, but I think that good will come of it for Texas. . . . I hope there will be no excitement about my arrest — it will do me harm and no good to Texas."

"I do not in any manner blame the government for arresting me," he wrote to the town council of San Felipe, "and I particularly request that there be no excitement about it. I give the advice to the people there that I have always given, keep quiet."

Next day they resumed their twenty-five day journey back to Mexico City. It was not too unpleasant. "I shall always be grateful for the courtesy with which General Lemus treated me," Austin said. "On the trip everything was furnished me. Nothing was wanting but liberty."

There were several prisons in Mexico City. Austin was taken to the most dreaded, the old stone prison of the Spanish Inquisition.

He was kept sitting on his horse in front of the prison while details of admitting him were arranged. Passers-by stared at him scornfully, and some of them jeered. Austin sat perfectly still, looking straight ahead. He could feel his face turning red and was angry that he should feel ashamed, for he knew that he was not a criminal.

Finally guards called him into the prison. They searched him and took away his personal belongings. But he managed to hide a small black notebook and a stub of pencil. Then they took a torch and led him down a long, winding passageway, dim and musty, to his cell.

He entered and stood waiting for his eyes to become accustomed to the darkness. He heard the heavy iron door slam shut. The key turned in the lock. Footsteps echoed for an instant in the passageway. Then everything was deathly still.

For the first time since his arrest six weeks before, Austin realized that he was actually a prisoner. The knowledge was very bitter.

His cell was a bare, high-ceilinged dungeon, thirteen feet by sixteen. The only light came from a small, dirty skylight high above. The stone walls and floor were cold and damp. There was no furniture, only a straw pallet to sleep on. There was a slot in the iron door. Through it, Austin could see only the stone wall opposite his cell. Later he learned that the slot was used for passing food to the prisoner.

He took the little notebook he had saved and his stub of pencil and wrote an entry for the day, February 13, 1834: "I was put in the inquisition, shut up in the dark dungeon No. 15 and not allowed communication with anyone."

What a few words when so many thoughts of worry, fear, and loneliness were twisting through his mind!

The next day he wrote, "I heard cannon which were fired at intervals all day as funeral honors to Guerrero, who was shot on Feb. 14, 1831."

The melancholy sound deepened his gloom. He could not help comparing his case with Guerrero's, for Guerrero had been a patriot too. Austin remembered Guerrero's decree abolishing slavery, a good decree, though it had caused so much trouble in Texas. Guerrero had been President of Mexico, but the people had turned against him and shot him to death. Austin could not help wondering, with a cold feeling at the pit of his stomach, whether he would meet the same fate.

On February 15 he wrote, "I was permitted to walk with a sentinel in a yard, alone, to take exercise. I asked for books but was not permitted to have any."

He was not permitted to speak to any of the other prisoners, either, though he sometimes saw them as they took their exercise. Nor was he permitted to write letters or see visitors. The only person he could talk to was the officer on guard, who would say only a few words to him.

Through this officer he arranged for his servant Medina to buy him a table and chair and to have his meals sent to him. But he could not learn what crime he was accused of or when his case would be tried.

Usually he kept the entries in his notebook brief and impersonal. But at times he grew so lonely and heartsick that he poured out his feelings in his little black journal.

"What a horrible punishment is solitary confinement, shut up in a dungeon with scarcely light enough to distinguish anything," he wrote on February 22. "If I were a criminal it would be another thing, but I am not one. . . . I do not see how I could have avoided what has passed in Texas; my conscience acquits me of anything wrong except impatience and imprudence. I am in no sense a criminal."

Next day he was allowed his first visitor, Father Muldoon, "who had great difficulty in obtaining this privilege," Austin wrote. "He was allowed to speak to me only in Spanish in the presence of the commandant of the prison. He promised to send me books."

On the twenty-fourth he continued, "I received my food according to Muldoon's promise but no books. I suppose he has not been permitted to send them. Time drags on heavily."

There was little he could do but sit and think, or pace the small cell restlessly. On sunny days about noon there was light enough in the cell to write in his journal or reread what he had written. He could see enough then also to examine the charcoal drawings on the walls of the dungeon, figures of snakes, landscapes, and other pictures drawn by a prisoner of the inquisition more than sixty years before.

He began to make a pet of a little mouse in the cell, too, and with a penknife made tiny models out of small sticks the guard let him have. But what a waste of time it seemed to a man whose days had been as crowded with work as Austin's had been.

One night he heard a rumbling noise and felt the prison shake. "Another revolution," he thought. "The prison must be under bombardment."

But there was no other noise. What had happened, he wondered helplessly.

At last the guard came with his breakfast and told him. "An earthquake, a bad one." But he hurried away without answering Austin's questions.

The next day Austin was awakened by another earthquake, even more severe than the one of the day before. After the first noise there was dead silence. Austin felt as frantic as a trapped animal. What if the quake had tumbled the outside walls of the prison? What if tons of rock sealed him in his cell and left him there to die?

After a long time the guard came. "How bad was the earthquake?" Austin asked.

"Very bad," the guard replied hurriedly. "Much damage. Houses toppled, people killed. Very bad!"

Austin spent the rest of the day in anxious waiting, but no more earthquakes shook the city.

On March 2 he wrote, "I obtained today a book — a tale called *Yes and No*. . . . I prefer bread and water with books to the best of eating without them. In a dungeon the mind and thought require aliment more than the body."

In the next three weeks he received three more books which helped to nourish his mind and thoughts. But his active mind needed more material than this to feed on.

He might have filled it with thoughts of hatred and revenge or of sorrow and self-pity and complaint. But he did not. Instead he filled it with plans for making Mexico and Texas better places in which to live.

Naturally, he tried to figure out why this imprisonment had happened, and he blamed himself for his impatience with Farias that day the bad news came from Texas and for his hasty letter. For years he had schooled himself to be patient, had urged his colonists to be patient. But in his grief and worry he had forgotten himself, with weeks of suffering as the result.

On April 13, just two months after his imprisonment began, thinking about his impatience and its consequences, he wrote: "In my first exploring trip to Texas in 1821 I had a very good old man with me, who was raised on the frontiers, a first rate hunter. We had not been many days in the wilderness before he told me, 'You are too impatient to make a good hunter.'

Scarcely a day passed that he did not say to me, 'You are too impatient — you wish to go too fast. I was so once but fifty years experience has learnt me that there is nothing in this world like patience.' "

It was very difficult to be patient in his dark, lonely dungeon. When he had been in solitary confinement for ten weeks, he wrote, "I know nothing of what passes outside. No one is allowed to speak to me, or I to anybody. . . . I do not know of what I am accused. How can I prepare my defense?"

About this time Santa Anna returned to Mexico City, and Vice-President Farias stepped aside. When Santa Anna learned of Austin's harsh imprisonment, he ordered it lightened. Austin was still a prisoner, but now he was allowed to talk to the other prisoners and to have the freedom of the cells and patio.

Austin was very grateful for this change, for being alone in the gloomy cell had been the hardest for him to bear. The other prisoners were also political prisoners, all army officers except two, who were priests. They were men of culture and respectability, and it was a blessed relief to have their company.

Santa Anna also allowed Austin to have visitors and to write to friends in Texas and Mexico.

By this time his money was almost gone, for even in prison he was required to pay for his food and other expenses. He let his servant go and no longer had good meals sent in from outside the prison. The dampness and chill of the stone walls and floor of the dungeon made him have frequent bad colds, and he began to suffer from rheumatism.

16:

Welcome Visitors

AFTER Austin had been in prison for three months, he thought that surely his case would be considered soon and he would be freed. But when his case finally came up, the court decided that it did not have power to try the case. Austin was moved to another prison, his case to another court.

After two more months this second court decided that it did not have jurisdiction either, and Austin was moved to a third prison, a dirty, shabby jail where he shared a cell with three Mexicans who were not political prisoners but actual criminals.

All this time Austin had received very few letters from Texas, and most of these were discouraging, hinting that he had enemies in Texas who were glad of his imprisonment.

He had asked that his arrest cause no excitement in Texas, for he wanted above all things to avoid a war. But he couldn't help feeling that after nine months the Texans' anger should be cooled enough so that they could help him without doing anything rash. When he had been allowed to write again, he had suggested that they could help him by writing that he had come to Mexico as their representative. But weeks and then months passed, and there was no word of help from Texas.

Austin still had friends in Mexico. Many of them visited him in prison after visitors were allowed. Some even tried unsuccessfully to persuade him to attempt to escape. Mostly they brought him alarming news. Some told him that it was believed that he had become immensely rich in Texas and had millions of dollars in United States banks, and that if he would pay the Mexican government fifty thousand dollars he would be set free. Of course, except for his Texas land, which would be of value only in the future, Austin was really quite poor. He could scarcely have raised five hundred dollars, certainly not a hundred times that much. Furthermore, he would not have bought his freedom in this way if he could, for it would seem like paying blackmail. He wanted his name cleared of all guilt.

Other visitors told him about enemies in Mexico who were trying to have him sent to the penal colony in California. Still others said that an important man was publicly demanding that Austin be shot.

And all this time there was nothing that Austin could do but sit in a damp, dirty cell and wait for the government to decide what his crime was and what court could try him — to wait and to write letters, letters to Mexicans explaining that he was not guilty of treason or a plot against Mexico, to Texans asking for their help.

He tried to stay patient and hopeful. But when eight months, nine months, passed without a word of help from Texas, he felt quite forsaken.

"My friends in Texas," he wrote to Samuel Williams, "may look on me as dead for a long time to come and probably forever. . . . Gen'l Santa Anna is friendly to me and so is the judge but what can they do against a host of bitter enemies which I made by opposing a territory, and others because I am a foreigner, and hundreds because I have been successful in settling Texas, and others from envy, and others because I am in misfortune. My situation is desolate — almost destitute of friends and money, in prison, amidst foes who are active to destroy me, and, forgotten at home by those I have faithfully labored to serve. I have been true and faithful to this nation; have tried to do all the good I could to individuals and the country. . . . I am now meeting my reward. I expect to die in this prison. It is hard and unjust and cruel. When I am dead justice will be done me. I have performed my duty and my conscience is at rest. . . . I have been the means of distributing millions of acres to make the fortunes of others, and I now doubt whether I shall not have to depend on charity for six feet of ground to sleep in at rest."

In the depths of hopelessness and loneliness he mailed this letter. A few days later the guards came to his cell. "Visitors for you," he announced.

Austin rose wearily from the straw mattress he was lying on. Two men pushed past the guard.

"Colonel Austin!" cried one man, rushing to him and grabbing his hand.

"Austin, old friend!" cried the other, throwing an arm around his shoulder.

"Grayson! Jack!" Austin exclaimed in joyous unbelief. "Is it you? Is it really friends from Texas?"

They saw that Austin was pale and thin from his long imprisonment, his face marked with lines of suffering, and they were moved with pity. He saw two friends from Texas: he was

not forgotten, he was not deserted. Try as he would, he could not keep the tears out of his eyes and the lump out of his throat, and Peter W. Grayson and Spencer H. Jack couldn't either. While Austin's Mexican cellmates watched curiously, the three men pumped each other's hands and pounded each other's backs and laughed to cover their emotions.

Presently Grayson and Jack explained that they brought petitions from Texas stating that Austin was acting as their representative, with no purpose of rebellion, and urging his immediate release. They said their coming had been delayed so long because they were afraid that anything they might try to do for him would only endanger him more.

Texans had never forgotten him, they said, or deserted him. As proof of their confidence in him, they brought official notice that the colonists had again elected him to represent them in the legislature.

Austin was greatly touched and pleased. In his happiness and relief it seemed that all his sufferings had been worth while since they led to this hour of recognition and faith.

Later that day he wrote accepting his re-election to the legislature: "No event of my life has afforded me more gratification — not because I desire office, or to have anything to do with public affairs. Far from it; I sincerely wish to avoid them. But situated as I now am, I should be worse than coldhearted and insensible not to feel the greatest degree of gratitude and thankfulness for this distinguished and unequivocal evidence of the confidence and esteem of my fellow citizens and laborers, because it is a vindication of what is dearer to me than life or liberty, my reputation."

Austin was as happy as if he had been set free. Indeed he felt that with Grayson and Jack, both good lawyers, working for his release, he would be free in a few days. But they soon found that they could not cope with the Mexican legal system and hired a Mexican lawyer to help them. Even so, it was not until Christmas Day of 1834 that Austin was released on bail.

Several lovely young girls who had been friends of Austin before his imprisonment were a great help in setting him free. One of them was from a wealthy family which had influence with Santa Anna. Another helped arrange for his bail.

After Austin was out of prison, he still was not free and could not leave Mexico City. Day by day his trial was delayed. Yet the six months before his final release were a happy time.

After his long days in prison everything in the world outside seemed fresh and interesting, and he found to his delight that he had more friends than ever before. The Mexicans admired his courage and patience, and Peter Grayson was telling of Austin's admirable behavior everywhere. "In the four months when I visited Austin in prison," he said, "I never heard him use an intemperate expression of any kind with respect to any person or circumstance connected with his imprisonment."

Such a forgiving spirit was rare, and his friends recognized it and with characteristic Mexican warmheartedness tried to make up for his sufferings by entertaining him in many ways.

Austin lived with a friend, George Hammekin, in Captain Washington W. West's hotel. He was popular there, too, and gained a nickname, "the Duke."

Austin felt that this time when he was free on bail, waiting his final release, was a lull in his life. He could not do any work for the colonists until he was back in Texas, and so for the first time since his college days he really relaxed and enjoyed himself. He attended dinners and balls, fiestas and plays, operas and concerts as the guest of various friends, and then he invited his friends to be his guests at affairs he thought they would enjoy.

He especially tried to show his appreciation to the young girls who had worked for his release. One opportunity occurred at the first balloon ascension in Mexico. The ascension, called an aeronaut, was a gala affair. The whole city was in a flutter of excitement about this amazing event, and a huge crowd turned out to witness it. Box seats for a choice place to observe the rising of the balloon sold at twenty dollars a ticket, and Austin was happy to give his young friends the pleasure of being present at this history-making event.

But, being Austin, he could not center all his activities on social affairs. Soon he was hard at work for Texas again, explaining to men of importance the plans he had recorded in his notebook in prison. Among them were the establishment of public mail service between Mexico and the United States, the encouragement of cotton manufacturing by building gins and mills in Mexico, the development of Galveston as a great seaport, and the building of many good roads. All were farsighted plans which eventually were carried out.

"I am happier than I have been for fourteen years," he wrote Williams. "My thoughts are now . . . beginning to confine themselves to . . . myself, my family, my own affairs. It is . . . a new life to me, for heretofore I have thought more of other matters than my own, but I shall soon get accustomed to it and be much happier."

His case never came to trial. Instead he was freed on June 22, 1835, under a law the Congress passed pardoning all political prisoners in Mexico. In July he left Mexico. He visited in New Orleans before his return to Texas; one thing he did there was to buy eleven books to take to Texas, a dictionary and books of travel, history, and biography. After his prison experience he never wanted to be without books again.

17:

War with Mexico

AUSTIN intended to wind up his colonization business in Texas, spend a year in traveling, and then return to Texas and settle down on a farm. But before he left New Orleans he heard news which made him realize that he would once again have to put aside his own plans and work for Texas.

He learned that after he had left Mexico, Santa Anna had overthrown the Mexican republic and set himself up as dictator. What was worse, Santa Anna had been very cruel in punishing one of the Mexican states that had dared to object to his dictatorship. He had sent soldiers to burn its cities, loot its homes, and shoot its leaders without mercy.

Austin knew that Texans would also object to Santa Anna's dictatorship. Almost certainly, Texas would be the next state to be punished. But Austin knew that if Santa Anna sent soldiers into Texas it would mean war, for the Texans would not submit to punishment without fighting back.

All these years Austin had worked hard to keep peace in Texas. His whole idea had been to conquer the wilderness and build a state by peaceful means. Could he prevent a war for Texas now? Should he try to prevent it?

Even before he had gone to Mexico two years ago, many Texans had wanted to settle their differences with Mexico by war. Sam Houston, a newcomer in Texas, and William Barret Travis, a young lawyer, were leaders of a group that thought Austin too cautious and timid in dealing with Mexico. He thought they were concerned more with winning glory for themselves as military heroes than with gaining the most for Texas pioneers, and he had convinced the majority of the settlers that they could get what they wanted by peaceful means.

Now he was not so sure that this could be done. His two years in Mexico dealing with politicians, his unjust imprisonment, the many false promises given him, made him doubt whether the Mexican government under Santa Anna could be trusted.

What would be best for Texas?

"To remain as we are," he had written to his old friend Mary Holley, "is impossible. We have not the right kind of material for an Independent Government, and a union with the United States would bring Negro Slavery, that curse of curses and worst of reproaches on civilized man. . . . I think the government will yield and give us what we ought to have. If not, we shall go for Independence and put our trust in ourselves, our rifles, and — our God."

Now it seemed clear that the government would not give them what they needed. Was war the only course left?

Austin made his position clear in a letter to Sam Houston. "In all our Texas affairs," he wrote, "I have felt it to be my duty to be very cautious in involving the pioneers and actual settlers of that country, by any act of mine, until I was clearly convinced of its necessity and of the capabilities of our resources to sustain it. Hence it is that I have been censured by some for being over-cautious. Where the fate of a whole people is in question, it is difficult to be overcautious, or to be too prudent."

On the voyage from New Orleans to Texas, Austin thought much about this Texas problem. He knew that many Texans would accept his decision in the matter. It was a heavy responsibility for him, but he comforted himself with the thought that he alone would not have to decide for Texas. After his long absence there would surely be others to whom the Texans would look for leadership.

But when he landed at the little port of Velasco, he learned that the decision of war or peace for Texas rested with him. The people gave him a welcome such as he had never dreamed of. They thronged to meet him, and welcomed him with tears and hugs and speeches. Some rode all night through rain and mud when they heard he had arrived. And the leading men of Texas who were far away wrote him letters of greeting.

F. W. Johnson wrote, "Your coming would always have been hailed by the people as the coming of a father, but your coming at this time is doubly dear to the people of Texas."

Gail Borden wrote to a friend about the feelings of joy and relief at Austin's return. He said that the colonists looked upon the event as one which would settle all their doubts as to what should be done and unite all parties. Even his enemies greeted him as the only physician who could restore Texas to a healthy condition.

"The people hail your appearance in Texas at this time as

one of the happiest events, because they believe you are capable of managing our difficult affairs better than we could without you," wrote another colonist.

William Barret Travis summed it up in his letter to Austin: "All eyes are turned to you. . . . Texas can be wielded by you and you alone; and her destiny is now in your hands."

The great welcome Austin met everywhere he went, coming only a few months after his despair and loneliness when he thought he was forgotten in prison, almost overwhelmed him with happiness. Yet it filled him with dismay, too, for he realized that the terrible decision of peace or war for Texas was his responsibility.

The people of Brazoria were giving a dinner and dance in his honor on September 8. He knew that he must announce his decision in his speech at the dinner. All the night before, he paced the beach at Velasco alone, considering the problem from every angle and praying for guidance.

His speech was a simple, quiet one. "My friends," he said, "I can truly say that no one has been, or is now, more anxious than myself to keep trouble away from this country. No one has been, or is now, more faithful to his duty as a Mexican citizen. But how can I, or any one, remain indifferent when our rights, our all, appear to be in jeopardy? It is impossible. The crisis is such that something must be done, and that without delay."

Everyone who heard him knew that he was declaring for war with Mexico. They accepted his decision without question.

At last all parties could unite in working for independence.

Of course there would be much to do first. Committees would meet and make plans, a convention would be called to accept these plans, and then the real work of building an army and a new government would begin.

A few days after his speech Austin received word that Mexican soldiers were landing on the Texas coast. By fast riders he sent a message to all the colonists: "War is our only resource. There is no other remedy but to defend our rights, ourselves, and our country by force of arms. To do this we must unite."

While the convention was being planned, Austin returned to San Felipe. In spite of the friendly welcome of people all along the way, his homecoming was forlorn, because he found his house with the chimney falling down, its rooms dusty and filled with cobwebs, and his furniture and personal belongings gone. He learned that friends and relatives had taken his furnishings, and he thought sadly that they must have given him up for dead in prison. But he set about briskly trying to get back his favorite possessions and buying others to start housekeeping again.

His sister and Mrs. Williams urged him to rent a room and board with someone in San Felipe. He would be more comfortable, they thought, and rid of the trouble of trying to keep bachelor hall. But Austin insisted on having his own home.

"It is a dog's life," he agreed, "but I am not yet a free man.

I am still a slave. I must be here to finish the land business and to try to systematize our political affairs. . . . There is much to do and it is of the greatest importance. . . .

"I must therefore have sheets and blankets and some other things and beds. . . . We must have private rooms to write in, far from noise or interruption. The formation of a government (perhaps of a nation) is to be sketched out. . . . A thousand things are to be done. But you will say that I ought not to be at all this expense. Have I not always been a packhorse? I must continue to be so a little while longer — and am willing to be so for the general good.

"I want a barrel of salt beef — 1 of salt pork. Two beds and bedding. Some spoons, some rice, some beans — send them by the steamboat. Also if Mrs. Williams can spare the oxen and wagon, I wish to keep it to haul wood until I can buy one. And some cows for milk, for I have nothing. I want a brick-layer to build the kitchen chimney, which has fallen down in the great rain, I would like to have one set of bed curtains. I must receive visitors and must be a little decent to receive them. I want hand irons for the fireplace and shovel and tongs. In fact, as housekeeping is a new thing, I hardly know what I want. . . . Among you, fit me out with something.

"As to the cost, it must go where the cost of my trip to Mexico went, and where I expect much more to go — that is, to serve the country. If that is well served, we shall all of us have enough, for we shall all prosper in common, and I shall be very well satisfied with that kind of compensation. I ask no other.

"Tell Emily I will attend to all my own private affairs as soon as I can, but the great cause of the country is the first thing."

Before he could get his house in order, he was called to the village of Gonzales. There Mexican soldiers had demanded the surrender of a small brass cannon which had been given to Gonzales as a protection against Indians. "Come and take it," the Texans had replied. As a result, the first battle of the war for independence was fought, and the Texans were victorious.

News of the fight spread quickly. When Austin arrived in Gonzales on October 11, he found four hundred men gathered to organize a Texas army, arguing and quarreling about what should be done and who should be the commander. Within a few hours they unanimously elected Austin their commander-in-chief.

Austin did not want this position. All he knew about military life had been learned when he was a member of the Arkansas militia in his youth, and at heart he was a man of peace, not a soldier. He felt he could do much more for Texas in working to get the army necessary food, equipment, and supplies instead of commanding it. Besides, he had just recovered from another illness and was still half sick.

But the men could not agree to serve under any other man, and they convinced Austin that it was his duty to unite them by becoming their commander-in-chief.

The main equipment of the army he commanded was courage. The soldiers had no uniforms. Most of the men wore

buckskin pants and coats, moccasins, and coonskin caps, and carried gourds for canteens. They had no regular ammunition. Each brought his own. Some had cap-and-ball pistols, others Spanish revolvers, still others long toms or muskets. Mostly they traveled on foot, but some in the group rode mules, others mustangs, and a few, thoroughbreds.

Each company chose its own captain, and the men expected him to do as they decided. These leaders, in turn, expected to be consulted by the commander-in-chief. It was a democratic but undisciplined army of less than a thousand men, but it was not afraid to face Santa Anna's tens of thousands.

Austin immediately led them to San Antonio, the main military center of the Mexicans, hoping to capture it before Mexican reinforcements could arrive. As they went along, he tried to bring military orderliness to the scattered band and to impress the men with the importance of obedience and co-operation.

On the way, his little force fought and won several skirmishes with the enemy. When they reached San Antonio, they camped outside the village and succeeded in keeping the Mexican forces there penned up. Austin wanted to storm San Antonio. He thought his men could take this important military post if they acted promptly. But the men voted against the attack.

On the bitterly cold morning of November 18, 1835, Moses Austin Bryan entered his uncle's makeshift headquarters. Austin, wrapped in a blanket for warmth, was seated on an upturned box, writing in his Order Book for the campaign.

"Uncle," began Moses. "I mean, General —"

"Uncle, when we are alone," Austin said with a smile.

"Well, then, Uncle, a messenger from San Felipe has just come with letters, one for you and one for me."

Each broke the seal on his letter and read in silence. When they had finished, Moses said, "Mine's from Mother. They're all well. Brother is going to join the army too."

"What does she say about little Stephen?" Austin asked eagerly.

"He's fine. One of Mr. Pilgrim's brightest pupils. But here, read for yourself," he offered.

"Good. We'll exchange."

Again each read silently, but only for a minute. "Why, Uncle," Moses exclaimed, "this says you're to resign as commander-in-chief. Why? Why?"

"If you'd read a little farther, you'd know," Austin replied calmly. "It's because the convention has selected me as a member of the commission to go to the United States to raise money for the war."

"But it isn't fair," Moses objected angrily. "Just when you are beginning to get the men to act like an army, it isn't fair to make you give up the command."

"I won't be sorry to leave. I'm not a military man, Moses."

"But you're doing a fine job. Nobody else could have held the men together the way you have."

"I'm not so sure. Look how they've voted me down about storming San Antonio."

"I'll admit they have voted against you on this," Moses agreed, "but what about Travis? He resigned because he was so angry when his men and officers refused to obey his orders. And what about Sam Houston? The men under him forced him to resign. But your men respect you. Your men have won victory after victory."

"Only small victories."

"But they're paving the way for the big ones. I still say it isn't fair to take the glory away from you after you have done the hard groundwork of building the army."

"You're young," Austin said, smiling again. "Military glory means more to you than it does to me. Ever since my first trip to Mexico I have been urging the people to play the turtle, keep head and feet in their own shell, to keep peace. But now we are in a war, and my only desire is to end it with victory as soon as possible. And such a victory will depend upon money for supplies. Unless the men are better supplied, the army will fall apart. You know how the men have been slipping away since this cold spell came."

"Yes. But most of them are going home to get warm clothes and a few good meals. They'll come back."

"Most of them will, yes, because I have promised them better food and more ammunition. But if that promise isn't kept, more and more men will be slipping off, and they won't return."

"I suppose you're right. It does take money to run a war."

"And weak and ill as I am, I feel that I am better suited to arranging loans for Texas than to leading her army."

"But, Uncle, if you go on this mission, you will be going north in the coldest part of the winter. Your health won't stand it."

"It's not exactly warm here," Austin replied drily, pulling his blanket closer.

"But this cold spell is very unusual for Texas. And it will be over in a few days. But in New York — you'll have to go to New York — it will be worse than this all the time."

"It won't be any worse for my health than camping with the army. However cold it may be, I'll have the comforts of civilization, remember."

"But —"

"If the people of Texas want me to go," Austin interrupted firmly, "I'll go if it kills me." He rose and walked toward his horse. "Help me mount my horse," he said. "I must tell the other officers about my new assignment."

"Who will succeed you as general?"

"Edward Burleson, I think."

"I'm afraid he won't be able to hold the men together."

"I'll talk to the men and get them to promise to stay. Now help me mount."

Moses helped him get on his horse. When he was in the saddle, Austin smiled down at his nephew ruefully. "When you think about it," he said, half sad, half joking, "it's a pretty sorry thing that the commander-in-chief of the Texas army is so weak and ill that he can't mount his horse by himself."

Moses reached up and squeezed his uncle's hand impulsively. "When you think about it," he said huskily, "it's a pretty magnificent thing!"

18:

The New Republic

THE day after Christmas, Austin, Dr. Branch T. Archer, and William H. Wharton set out on their mission to raise money in the United States. As he stood at the rail of the steamship and watched the shores of Texas disappear in the distance, Austin remembered how many of the important events of his life had happened during the Christmas season. It was on Christmas that his father had accidentally met Baron de Bastrop and thereby received permission to start Texas colonization. It was on New Year's Eve the following year that Austin had arrived in Texas with the first settlers. It was on December 29, 1829, that Austin learned that his colony was exempt from the Emancipation Decree, which would have ruined it financially. During the Christmas season of 1833 he was on his way home from Mexico, not knowing that the messenger with the order for his arrest would overtake him at Saltillo. The following year he was freed from prison on Christmas Day. Now, a year later, he was setting out to get life-or-death support for Texas.

His heart was unhappy with fears and doubts this year. He was afraid he could not work well with the other commissioners, who had been his political enemies; afraid that his health would fail, leaving him unable to do his share of the work. And he doubted that bankers would be willing to risk money on the uncertain future of Texas.

But the mission was more successful than Austin expected. At their very first attempt to borrow money, in New Orleans, they made a loan of two hundred and fifty thousand dollars, receiving sixty thousand dollars in cash. With this they immediately bought the supplies so badly needed by the Texas army.

Encouraged, they traveled to Washington, stopping at important cities along the way to meet with bankers and businessmen to arrange for more money for Texas. They also attended many dinners and meetings where they made speeches to arouse interest in Texas' struggle for independence.

As they worked together and grew to know one another better, the three men became good friends. Before they reached Washington, Austin became ill, but after several weeks he was able to rejoin the other commissioners and then go on by himself to New York. There he arranged for a loan of a hundred thousand dollars.

The commissioners could have borrowed much more of the desperately needed money if they had had regular official news from Texas. But during all the time they were in the United States they had no letter from the president of Texas, none from the general of her armies, or from any other official.

News about Texas appeared in the newspapers of the United States, but it was weeks old by the time it reached print. Besides, it was all discouraging. First there was the tragic story of the fall of the Alamo, where every one of its defenders died fighting rather than surrender. Then there was the shocking account of the massacre at Goliad. Soon there was news of the frightened flight of women and children and old men to reach the safety of the United States, and of the alarming retreat of Sam Houston's army before the pursuing soldiers of Santa Anna.

All this news aroused a great deal of sympathy for Texas, and hundreds of volunteers marched off to help in the heroic struggle for freedom. But it was not the kind of news that encouraged businessmen to risk their money on Texas. "How can a few hundred Texans win over Mexico's thousands?" they asked. "How do we know that Texas is not already defeated?"

Austin was so sure of victory that he pledged all his land as security for the money he borrowed. After he heard of the fall of the Alamo, he wrote, "My heart and soul are sick, but my spirit is unbroken. Santa Anna has raised the bloody flag of a pirate — the fate of pirates will sooner or later be his fate. . . . Texas will rise again."

All three of the commissioners lived in worry and uncertainty, and dread of what sad news they would hear next.

At last, a month after it had happened, the papers carried the glorious news of Texas victory at San Jacinto, of Santa Anna's surrender to Sam Houston.

Texas independence was won, but Texas needed more money to carry on the affairs of a new nation. Businessmen were more sympathetic now, but before they would agree to lend money, they wanted to know whether Mexico would send another army against Texas; they wanted all the facts about conditions there.

The commissioners could not give them these facts because they still had no official word. So, feeling that they had done all they could and had at least prepared the way for future loans, they returned home.

Austin landed at Velasco late in the afternoon of June 27, and before nightfall he was busy working for Texas again. A conference with President Burnet and conversations with others led him to fear that Mexico might make another attempt to conquer Texas.

This attempt would depend on Santa Anna. He was a prisoner now, but only because volunteers under General Lamar refused to let him sail for Vera Cruz, as the government had ordered. For according to the treaty made with General Houston and President Burnet, Santa Anna was to be set free. If he were set free, he might break his promise as he had so often done before, and try again to defeat Texas. If he were put to death, as many Texans demanded, the new president of Mexico might

send an army to avenge his death.

"Texas was saved by the victory at San Jacinto," Austin wrote that night, "and almost lost by the armistice made in the moment of victory with a prisoner."

He worked out a plan to use Santa Anna to help gain Texas recognition by the United States. He persuaded Santa Anna to write a letter to President Jackson stating that Mexico could not conquer Texas and should recognize her as independent. Later Santa Anna was sent under escort to the United States to convince the President that Mexico had no further claims on Texas, and then he was set free to return to Mexico.

At first Austin was criticized for saving Santa Anna's life, but as time went by, almost everyone agreed that his plan had saved Texas from another invasion, besides making it possible for the United States to recognize Texas independence.

On July 20 the commissioners met in Velasco to wind up their business. When they had finished, they sat back in their chairs, relaxed.

"Well, on the whole, we did pretty well," Wharton concluded.

"We might have done better if the government had kept us informed," Austin replied. "However, I have the president's solemn promise to keep the new commissioners constantly informed about developments in Texas."

"That will make their task easier," said Dr. Archer, "but I'm glad they're sending a new group instead of asking us to go again."

"So am I," Austin agreed heartily. "Well, gentlemen, this ends my public work for Texas. At last I am just a private citizen."

Austin saw Wharton and Dr. Archer look at each other significantly. Uneasily, he sat straighter in his chair.

"Austin," said Dr. Archer, "there's to be an election for the first president of the Republic of Texas. Have you thought of becoming a candidate?"

"Not I," Austin answered quickly. "I detest politics. I always have, and my recent experience with politicians in Mexico did nothing to change my opinion."

"But think of the honor, man," Wharton urged. "To be the first president of the Republic! It's an honor you have earned."

"I don't want it," Austin replied positively. "My ambition was to redeem Texas from the wilderness, to settle it with intelligent, honorable, and enterprising people. I probably shall not live to derive much personal benefit, but I have greatly benefited many others and made them and their families rich, who were worth nothing before, and I have opened and enlarged a fine field for human enterprise. Now I want only to live in peace and quiet as a private citizen."

"Austin, have you ever thought that it is your duty to run for the presidency?"

"Duty! Duty!" Austin exclaimed wearily. "For fifteen years I have done my duty to Texas and neglected my own affairs. I am tired of doing my duty, tired in body and soul. I need to relax and rest. I want a chance to do the things for myself I have put off for so long. I want to travel for a while and then to settle down on a farm next to my sister with little Stephen as my son. To look around for a wife, perhaps. Let others think of duty for a change."

"But this is a crisis, Austin," Wharton continued. "Think of it, man, a new nation on the face of the earth, a nation with a destiny of greatness! Shall that nation die because the wrong person has it in charge?"

"There are others who could lead it. I am not the only one."

"You are the best one," Dr. Archer said quietly. "Who else

has been president of Texas in everything but name all these years? Who else knows her problems, her needs, her resources, as you do?"

"What makes you so sure I'd be elected if I ran?"

"The people have confidence in you. Remember how they flocked to you when you returned from Mexico?"

"Austin," Wharton continued quickly, "what is the first problem of the new nation?"

"Recognition by the United States, of course, and then annexation to the United States. You know that. Unless the United States recognizes Texas as an independent nation, Mexico will soon send another army against us. Unless the United States recognizes Texas, there will be no way for us to borrow money to finance our nation."

"Exactly," Wharton agreed. He took a handful of letters from his briefcase. "And here are letters from prominent men in the United States urging that you become the president of Texas. You are the one who can get this vital recognition from the United States."

Austin took the letters and read them in silence. When he had finished, he turned to William Wharton. "Wharton, do you sincerely think it is my duty to run for president?" he asked.

"I do," Wharton replied firmly.

"Dr. Archer, do you think it is my duty?"

"Yes, Austin, I do."

"Then," Austin said quietly, "I will become a candidate."

19:

Father of Texas

THE campaign proved to be a very bitter one, with lies and personal attacks against Austin.

"Tell John to keep clear of land speculators," Austin had written from Mexico in 1833. "I had rather deal with devils than with that class of mankind."

But while Austin was in prison, his secretary, Samuel Williams, had not kept clear of land speculators, and now political enemies falsely accused Austin of having made huge dishonest profits in land speculation with Williams.

All these attacks and accusations by the settlers he had befriended for so many years hurt Austin deeply. He realized it was all a part of the politics he had despised all his life; yet it made him heartsick. By speeches and letters printed in the newspapers he tried hard to convince the voters of his honesty and asked them to prove their faith in him by electing him.

But, just a few weeks before the election, Sam Houston announced himself a candidate for the presidency.

Sam Houston was a big, handsome, forceful man. At fourteen he had run away from home to live with the Cherokee Indians. Later he fought in the American army under Andrew Jackson and became Jackson's personal friend. A few years later he was elected governor of Tennessee but suddenly resigned and returned to live with the Cherokees. In 1832 he had come to Texas and for the four years since then had taken an active part in Texas politics and warfare. Letters indicated that he once planned to make himself emperor of Texas.

Everything he did appealed to the imagination of people and made him seem heroic. Even the way he dressed was romantic. Sometimes he wore the colorful blanket, feathers, and beads of the Cherokees, sometimes the simple homespun and buckskin of the pioneers, at other times the fine linen and broadcloth of a fashionable gentleman. He had a dramatic way of talking, too, and when he made a speech, it was a genuine spellbinder. Most of all, as commander-in-chief of the Texas army, he had won independence for Texas.

As soon as Houston entered the race, Austin knew that he would not be elected. Except that his election would have publicly cleared his name, he was not disappointed, and in spite of the sharp hurt of being lied about by his colonists, he took the matter calmly.

"I feel but little anxiety, of a personal character, whether I am elected or not," he said. Long ago he had written, "The sovereign people are the hardest taskmasters on earth." Another time he had said, "You know it is innate in an American to suspect and abuse a public officer whether he deserves it or not." He realized, too, that he had enemies, for as he said, "None but a miserable and contemptible poor devil could have had as much to do with public matters as I have in Texas without making enemies."

What hurt him most was the thought that his good friend Sam Williams had betrayed him in the land speculations. But Williams wrote him a letter asking forgiveness, and Austin replied, "Williams, you have wounded me very deeply, but you are so deeply rooted in my affections, that with all your faults, you are at heart too much like a wild and heedless brother to be entirely banished. Come home."

Three days before the election, Austin wrote his brother-in-law about building a two-room cabin and furnishing it for him. "These arrangements are made on the supposition that I shall not be elected," he concluded. "So that I have a good prospect of some rest this year and time to regulate my private affairs, which need regulating very much."

As Austin had expected, Houston won an overwhelming victory in the election. Austin prepared to go about his own business at last, but an attack of malaria delayed him.

When, as Austin expressed it, he was "barely able to crawl about" again, Houston asked him to become his secretary of

state. This was the most difficult position in the new republic, and everyone admitted that Austin was the best man for it. No one else had his knowledge of Texas and its problems and of affairs in Mexico and the United States as well. But Austin refused.

"I have all the land office business to close," he said. "Besides all this, my health is gone, and I must have rest."

But Houston begged him to reconsider and finally persuaded him that by accepting this position in the cabinet, he could not only secure the vital recognition from the United States but also heal the bitterness resulting from the campaign and again unite Texas.

And so once more Austin put the interest of Texas above his own. Once more he laid aside his plans for a farm and became the first secretary of state of the Republic of Texas.

If on his return from prison there had been a hundred things to do, there were a thousand now, in setting up the government of a new nation and gaining recognition for that government from the United States and other countries of the world.

The new capital of Texas was in Columbia, where a log cabin served as the capitol building. Austin stayed in a two-room cabin at the home of his friend George B. McKinstry, riding to work on a mule until he could find a horse that suited him.

There were so many things to plan, so many letters to write, so many people to see, that Austin worked day and night. Much of the time he was weak and ill, but on November 3 he wrote to Sam Williams, "This is my birthday. My health is much improved, though still bad. . . . The public matters are getting on well. A state of things which I have long labored to bring about is gradually coming round."

He was happy in his work, even though it left him utterly exhausted, and he began again to plan for his own future. His dream of a little farm seemed very near now. Perhaps by spring the United States would recognize the independence of Texas. Then his public work would indeed be ended. He would be free to resign as secretary of state and devote his time to building his small home and surrounding it with his favorite shrubs and trees.

With this in mind, early in December he sent a collection of seeds and young trees to Perry with instructions for planting them on their land.

He was lonely for a home, for the rest and comfort and companionship a home would bring. Ever since he had set out for Mexico in April, 1833, he had been without a place of his own.

"I have no house, not a roof in all Texas that I can call my own," he wrote at this time. "The only one I had was burned at San Felipe during the late invasion of the enemy. I make my home where the business of the country calls me. . . . I have no farm, no cotton plantation, no income, no money, no comforts. I have spent the prime of my life and worn out my constitution in trying to colonize this country. Many persons boast of their 300 and 400 leagues acquired by speculation without personal labor or the sacrifice of years or even days; I shall be content to save 20 leagues or 90,000 acres, acquired very hard indeed. All my wealth is prospective and contingent upon events of the future. What I have been able to realize in active means has gone . . . where my health and strength and time have gone, which is in the service of Texas, and I am therefore not ashamed of my poverty."

And so the Christmas season came around again, and Austin's old friend from Mexico City, George L. Hammekin, came to see him.

Austin was sick in bed with a cold and fever, but he was glad to see Hammekin. The visit made him forget his aches and worries and remember the pleasant times of his last weeks in Mexico when he and Hammekin and his other friends had been carefree together, and had joked and laughed and danced and listened to music.

"I'll find you some place in the government," Austin told

Hammekin, "and I'll let you have some of my stock. They say it will be valuable some day."

"No, Duke," Hammekin replied gently, using Austin's Mexico nickname. "I haven't come to get this time, but to give. I heard about your position in the government and wondered whether I couldn't help you with your personal business affairs."

"That will suit me exactly," Austin said, smiling. "I need help badly. When I get better, we'll talk about it."

But Austin didn't get better. The day after Christmas he developed pneumonia. His friends knew he was very ill and sent for his sister.

Because there was no fireplace in his bedroom, Austin spread a pallet near the fireplace in his office and lay on the floor. When he could, he sat at his table, wrapped in blankets, resting his head on his arms, for he could breathe easier in that position. But he was too weak to sit up long.

Early in the morning of December 27, Perry and one of Austin's nephews came. The doctor told them of a remedy that would be Austin's only chance of getting well, but in his weakened condition might prove fatal. They decided to take the chance.

After the treatment Austin whispered faintly, "Now I will go to sleep."

In a little while he woke up and said with a happy smile, "Texas recognized! Archer told me so. Did you see it in the papers?"

It was only a feverish fancy, of course, for it was months

before the United States did recognize Texas. But it made Austin's last moments happy. He sank back, and in a few minutes Sam Houston announced solemnly to the Texas Congress, "The Father of Texas is no more."

Austin's dream of a quiet home on a little farm never did come true, but his greater dreams for Texas did. And in his lifetime he had the calm, deep joy of knowing that this was so.

"I have not made a fortune for myself," he said, "but I have benefited many others, hundreds of them. . . ."

What made Austin's work different from that of Captain John Smith or Daniel Boone or any of the other American pioneers? They all faced the same dangers and hardships of the "howling wilderness" and conquered them, but two things made Austin's task harder. For one thing the other American pioneers from Pilgrim times on came to a land where there was no government. They either made their own laws and government or brought it with them. And they were usually encouraged and aided by the government that sent them. Austin took his colonists into a land governed by a foreign nation which had a kind of government very different from the American system, a nation whose people were unfriendly and suspicious toward North Americans. Besides this, the Spanish language, ideals and customs of everyday living were strange to his people.

Because of these differences Austin's problem was not only to subdue the wilderness but also to keep peace between his settlers and their adopted country, Mexico. He succeeded, though during his fourteen years in Texas, Mexico was torn by almost constant rebellions and revolutions.

His success was not due to chance. He foresaw the difficulties and planned carefully to overcome them. "My first step was to study the character of the Mexicans and ascertain their views as to Texas," he explained. "These observations convinced me that the only way of redeeming this country from the wilderness was by peaceful, silent, noiseless perseverance and industry, and that the axe, the plough, and the hoe would do more than the rifle and the sword."

It may be thought that the time was ripe for settling Texas, that anyone trying to colonize Texas at that time would have succeeded. But history shows that this is not true, for several attempts to colonize Texas with North Americans before Austin's ended in failure, and some of the *empresarios* who came to Texas after Austin's colony was started failed too.

At first Austin did not intend to make Texas a part of the United States. He was sincere in his desire to make it a great state of Mexico. But he recognized faults in the Mexican system of the time and considered it his patriotic duty to avoid these faults in his colony. Consequently, quietly but forcefully, he worked to include the features of American life he thought most necessary for a good government and a prosperous people. Among these were power divided among departments of the government instead of held by one person, free elections, trial by jury, public education, and newspapers to keep the citizens informed.

Until Austin's imprisonment in Mexico he thought that an Americanized, self-governed state of Texas could be a strong state in the Mexican union. After that time he felt that Texas must be independent of Mexico.

Not many of the Texans of his day were farsighted enough to realize the full importance of Austin's work. He took this public indifference calmly. "The bloodless pioneer of the wilderness," he once said, "like the corn and cotton he causes to spring where it never grew before, attracts no notice." When his sister complained about the lack of gratitude of the settlers, he replied, "In the end they will be just and if I merit a reward from them, they will give it. The settlers of this colony will never forget the man or the family who has made their fortunes."

Texans never have forgotten Austin. On the banks of the Colorado, on land he selected for a home but never owned in his lifetime, is the beautiful city named for him, Austin, the capital of Texas. And there, where he planned to found an academy, is the great University of Texas.